Ox Herding: A Secular Pilgrimage

JACKIE GRIFFITHS

Dedication

This book is dedicated to Brian Nicholson, door-opener extraordinaire and life-long mentor.

For Saskia, Freddy, and Genevieve.

Contents

Acknowledgments

I would like to thank Chris Purchase, Malcolm MacDonald, & Ally Wrenn for their invaluable contributions.

Prologue

Although those close to her say she's been acting strangely for several months, the death of Jae's grandmother propels her into a deeper, more permanent state of despondency. If someone compliments her, she feels embarrassed and hastily downplays whatever it is the other person has praised. If someone criticises her, her stomach tenses with anger and defensive counter-arguments fly uncontrollably out of her mouth. When she catches sight of a vase of tulips radiant in the full light of the sun, their beauty doesn't inspire or calm her; instead she becomes fretful and wants to talk. While this anomalous mood of irritability and introversion does seem to have become worse since the bereavement, deep down, Jae knows a fundamental discontent has been developing for much longer, and lately it's been intensifying to such an extent that she's starting to feel overwhelmed.

Since her early teenage years she'd felt a special kinship with her paternal grandmother, convinced they shared a unique and profound alliance of philosophical and political affinity. Vivian was ahead of her time; a sprightly, upright octogenarian of dubious moral conviction (according to Jae's parents). She'd gone to university in the days when it was unusual for women to continue in further education. She hadn't married until her late thirties, and had refused to give up her career after having a baby at nearly forty. Jae had always admired her choices and apparent unwavering self-belief. She was the kind of person who never just went along with what was expected of her by society, but instead researched the issue and made up her own mind. Secretly Jae believes that Vivian has passed this streak of defiance and courage on to her, skipping her father's generation.

They'd had many extraordinary conversations over the years on a variety of complex topics, including philosophy, politics, and religion, but her granny had also been able to advise her on more trivial aspects of life. In Vivian, Jae had found both a friend and mentor, and although they had only managed to see each other about once a month, they'd forged a deep and affectionate bond.

When, about a month ago, she had died suddenly and peacefully during the night, it was surprisingly unexpected and traumatic for Jae, despite the fact that at eighty-six years of age such an event is not inconceivable. Jae came to realise that no matter how much you mentally prepare for the death of a loved one, when it actually happens it's a completely different proposition, full of unforeseeable emotional distress and practical complications.

Vivian had left Jae a small sum of money - not sufficient to put down as a deposit for a house, but enough to, perhaps, start a business, or finally move out of her parent's house, rent a flat and live comfortably for a year without stress. However, at present, Jae can't gather her thoughts into enough order or clarity to be able to make a decision. She feels she needs more time to grieve and recuperate after the death of her dear friend. So she simply continues to live with her parents in emotional suspension, feeling incomplete, unresolved, lacking the ability to concentrate on any one topic for long.

But far more disconcerting for Jae than the question of what to do with the money, is that in her will, Vivian had also left her a most peculiar little note. At first it had seemed fairly innocuous, perhaps an oblique reference to a previous conversation, but it continued to linger in Jae's mind, stuck like a blob of glue, interfering and intruding persistently into her thoughts. She's sure her grandmother must have meant something quite specific that she can't, at present, fathom.

A few weeks after her grandmother's death she had received a letter from the solicitor informing her of the sum of her inheritance, along with a cheque, plus a small sealed white envelope. Inside was a folded piece of paper on which had been handwritten in her grandmother's wobbly scrawl just one single line:

'Seek and ye shall find.'

Perplexed as to why her grandmother, a life-long

agnostic, would leave her a religious quote, Jae hadn't yet been able to decipher what it meant.

Many times they had discussed spiritual issues together during long, sunny afternoons over endless cups of green tea and homemade banana cake. Vivian would sit upright and alert in her pale-green, wing-backed armchair, becoming ever more animated as she talked, while Jae squatted on a footstool at her feet, holding her plate under her chin to avoid scattering crumbs on the rug. However, there was never any suggestion of her converting to Christianity or to any other religion, nor of trying to convert Jae to any kind of belief. But perhaps, in the last few weeks, Vivian had somehow sensed her impending end and had finally found a spiritual conviction?

But because it goes completely against the grain, contradicting the memory of the woman she knew so well, it's a riddle Jae can't resolve. Brooding on it almost hourly, she feels her life sliding into an inescapable state of abeyance, the strange message from her granny nagging relentlessly away at the edge of her consciousness. She feels helplessly suspended in a frustrating state of uncertainty and confusion, yet knows that as each week slowly passes, and she continues to allow herself to capsize into a morass of inner turmoil, it will eventually become a very costly surrender. The need to resolve her intellectual crisis has reached near breaking point.

CHAPTER ONE

The First Stirring of the Heart

One morning, waking earlier than usual and staring out of the bedroom window, Jae feels a rush of resentment for the bare branches of an old magnolia tree in the front garden. As spring approaches, it has become her habit to check each morning for buds - within which hairy little capsules lie dormant a brief yet magnificent blossoming. She's learnt that when those flame-like shoots of concentrated energy appear on the twigs, an extraordinary process will commence within the tree that, in due course, will generate a wondrous vision with the capacity to restore her soul. For the ensuing precious few weeks of full bloom, the first thing she'll see each day will be a view filled with such a profusion of exquisite pastel shades of pink, that she'll have the impression of rousing from sleep in the Garden of Eden itself.

For some reason this year she desperately awaits sight of their glory, sensing it will somehow salvage her spirit; rescue her life force from the wilderness and deliver her into a long hoped-for equanimity. But when, each morning, the branches continue to show no signs of life, she feels a kind of rage as if a great personal injustice has been meted out.

Today, as usual, there's nothing new to see. Slumping back onto the bed she imagines the barren, lacklustre tree perfectly symbolises her life at present. Closing her eyes again she tries unsuccessfully to go back to sleep. Living with her parents and five-year-old daughter in a pleasant detached house in an unremarkable village, her life just bumbling along one day very much the same as the next, is starting to feel extremely mundane and repetitive. She knows she has the potential to do, and be, so much more in life, but has become bogged down in the quicksand of averageness, of humiliating mediocrity, and is slowly suffocating to death. Her life feels increasingly wasted, without point or purpose. Opening her eyes and giving up on any more sleep, she thinks: *the tree and I are both in suspension, preserved in a wintery catatonia, waiting in silence to blossom. But what if I never do?*

Sluggishly getting up and heading for the bathroom, she hunches gloomily on the toilet reconciling herself to being awake. Her long brown hair straggles untidily down her back, and she notices her Flashing Lilac nail varnish is chipped and needs to come off. Feeling strangely unsettled, she retraces her steps back to the bedroom, picks up her iPad and makes her way unsteadily downstairs to switch the kettle on. Huddling into her dressing gown she tries to keep warm while scrolling down her Facebook newsfeed.

As the kettle approaches boiling point she looks at the steam erupting furiously into the air and broods, *there must be something more than this monotonous, predictable life. Does anything I do mean anything?* Pouring water into a cup she glances at her reflection in the side of the kettle. A hideous gargoyle stares obstinately back.

Agitating her teabag in the water it seems to Jae as if she's experiencing life from a hazy distance, as though she's standing behind a window pane covered in raindrops while everything takes place on the other side, blurred and remote. Squeezing the teabag against the side of the cup she thinks, *I want to find peace within myself again; to be settled and content with everything, like I used to be.* After months of confusion and ambivalence, more than anything, she wants clarity, peace, and for the questions to stop.

A few minutes later, after eating a boiled egg and hot buttered toast, Jae's mood lifts at last. Breakfast has infused her with renewed energy and a change of heart. *Perhaps I just need to eat more,* she thinks walking back upstairs more confidently. Opening a bedroom door and entering the room without taking care to be quiet, she gently shakes her daughter awake. "Chloe, time to wake up now my darling. Leaving for school in forty-five minutes."

On the walk back from school along the river, Jae's feelings of disquiet return and she fleetingly wonders whether she might be depressed. No-one she knows is ill, destitute, or greatly suffering. No-one's dying, been made redundant, just had a car crash or been attacked on the street. So many awful things can happen to people every day, and yet Jae's life is perfectly normal and calm. Her parents are decent, kind, and supportive; her daughter is a happy, healthy, popular girl. Her friends and boyfriend appear to love her… so why does she feel something vitally important is missing?

She can't explain her strange thoughts and lingering yearning for a state or way of being she can't even name. As she drifts through her life these days, she feels deeply dissatisfied with everything.

She thinks, *maybe it's because I don't have a career?*

However, deep down, she agrees with the choice she made five years ago not to work until her baby was old enough to be in full-time school. And although the three of them had started off living together in Justin's one-bed flat, it became too cramped and difficult to continue; so when her parents offered a temporary solution to accommodate Jae and Chloe back in the family home, it suited everyone: Justin remained in his flat; Jae and Chloe stayed nearby (moving only to the next village) and her parents were able to enjoy daily contact with their only grandchild.

Justin and Jae didn't split up as a couple; they simply altered their living arrangements. And although they now see less of each other than they used to, it's better quality time when they do get together – which Jae believes they all benefit from. So although temporarily assuaged while focusing on the move, this adaption in her living setup didn't pacify her underlying mood of dissatisfaction in the long-term.

A collection of Jae's personal property - small pieces of furniture, mirrors, paintings and various knickknacks - are now scattered throughout her parents' house in random positions; some stored in the wardrobe in Chloe's room, but the majority in her bedroom cluttering shelves and stacked untidily in corners. One day soon she needs to go through everything and create piles of items to keep, give away, and dump. She has far too many possessions that she doesn't really need, or even like that much, but which for some reason she feels loathe to part with. You never know when you might need a large straw hat, a tall purple glass bottle with matching stopper, three spare mirrors, or a pleasant oil painting of a pastoral scene with a cow and herder...

If only she didn't feel so odd half the time, as if she's missing out, or lacking something; as if a whole other world were out there that she's not seeing or participating in. It seems to Jae as if there must be a wonderful mystery, some kind of sacred spirituality to life just waiting to be discovered - except that as she moves through her daily existence, taking care of Chloe, attending choir practice, doing housework and being with Justin, there plainly isn't any mystery anywhere.

It's as if I've lost something mysterious or profound but I've no idea what, she muses carefully stepping over a muddy puddle on the towpath, as she continues her walk home from school. *How can I begin to search for something if I don't know what it is I've lost? Or even whether I've lost anything in the first place...* Her thoughts mill around loosely and aimlessly in her head like passengers on a railway concourse. Not for the last time she misses her granny and their many fascinating and revitalising conversations.

She sighs deeply, avoiding some overgrown

stinging nettles, and continues making guesses at what's lacking in her life that could explain her yearning, empty feelings. She composes a list in her head:

No career.
No religion.
Living at home.
No purpose.

Any one of these alone could be the problem. Her parents are Christian and seem to find all the extra meaning they need from their religion. *I'm of no religion.*

Her friends talk about their jobs, frequently stating they'd "go mad" if they weren't able to get out of the house, work, and earn money. *I have no job. I don't earn any money.* Jae stops to stare across the fields. But in reality not having a career doesn't trouble her very much. *But should it? Why doesn't being jobless bother me when it bothers everyone else?*

Turning to gaze at the river, she loses herself in the swirls and patterns forming in both her mind and the water. Family and friends accuse her of thinking too much, which she readily acknowledges is true, but her urgent questions just won't go away. She can't seem to turn her thoughts off. They feel strangely vital, as if her life itself somehow hinged on them, or their answers. They arise in each pause, in each silence, creating their own noise and confusion, unbidden. *I know I think too much – I can't help it! I'm searching for something but I'm blind, searching in the dark...*

Forlornly, she reflects that although her grandmother has died, life still goes on for everyone else. The world still turns, people still get up and go to work as usual, regardless of another's pain or loss. *How can the death of someone you love so much have no impact whatsoever on the world?* She feels helpless and upset in the face of this fact - a person quietly flickering out of existence, disappearing from life forever and the world just continuing the same as it always has, without even a pause. It seems wrong.

So perhaps all this mental turmoil is simply the normal effect of grief? This may be partly the case, but in truth Jae knows her aggravated state of mind gradually came into existence during the months **before** her grandmother died.

Turning away from the river and proceeding along the slightly muddy path, she imagines what her mother would say about her current mood. "You need to **do** something, Jae, have a purpose in life; goals, aims, things to occupy you. All you really accomplish is thinking, singing, and taking care of Chloe! There are an awful lot of other things out there you could be doing."

But to Jae such suggestions sound wasteful, disrespectful, as if time were something to be filled or occupied for no purpose other than distraction itself. Shouldn't life be worth living anyway, without deliberately fluffing it up and plumping it out with activities just for the sake of it?

No. She feels she can't accept her life continuing on as it presently is. However, knowing beyond doubt what she doesn't want isn't the same as knowing or understanding what she does.

As always when she ponders the big life questions, which these days seems to be hourly, she ends up without a conclusion, dismissing everything as purely anxiety or stress. She can't seem to order the questions enough to see what they are, if indeed there are a number of different questions. *Perhaps*, she conjectures, *there is really only one fundamental question masquerading as many by means of repeated refraction through innumerable prisms in my mind?*

Back home, Jae inserts her key into the lock, opens the front door and steps inside the silent, empty house.

Rising the next morning, resolutely ignoring the dead-looking magnolia waving provocatively at her in slow-motion outside the window, Jae picks up her iPad and makes a quick visit to the bathroom, before staggering downstairs to get the kettle going. Her newsfeed reveals new statuses, debates, photographs, and various events that have occurred since she previously looked eight hours ago, before falling asleep last night. Nibbling toast and sipping tea she sits at the kitchen table to check her email.

Upstairs, twenty minutes later, she enters her daughter's room, kisses her awake, and helps her get ready for school.

Today is starting off the same as every other day of the week, but at least this evening Jae will do something just for herself. Singing once a week at choir is her special and greatly-anticipated enjoyment. They're rehearsing Beethoven's Mass in C Major and this evening they'll be working on the Gloria, the second movement of the piece. 'Glory be to God in the highest and peace on earth to men of good will.' All very traditional, but Jae prefers the sounds of the words in Latin: 'Gloria in excelsis Deo et in terra pax hominibus bonae voluntatis.' Somehow, the overall feeling of the music is more emotive and inspiring when she's singing in such a foreign and evocative language.

Although not generally considered to be among Beethoven's greatest works, some critics concede the Mass in C Major has been unfairly overlooked, perhaps overshadowed by the great Missa Solemnis he composed some fifteen years later. However Jae finds it very beautiful, and this evening to her amazement becomes moved beyond reason while listening to the soloists sing the 'qui tollis peccata mundi, suscipe deprecationem nostram' section – ('You who take away the sins of the world, hear our prayers'). Standing in the second row from the front in the soprano section, she casts worried glances around the room. *Maybe I'm having a nervous breakdown,* she panics, surreptitiously flicking a few tears from her face and hoping no-one notices her over-emotional state. *This isn't normal.*

That night she dreams of a strange man with short dark hair riding high on the back of a powerful black ox. They thunder towards her from the wilderness, trampling beautiful herbs and wild flowers underfoot. Slowing as they approach, man and beast come to a halt about a metre away from Jae.

Blazing down at her from between the enormous horns of the powerful creature the man shouts, "who are you kidding? You haven't found any path yet, let alone pathlessness."

"But I'm trying so hard…" replies Jae, anguished.

"You get what you deserve, whether you deserve it or not!" replies the man bewilderingly, before raising his whip, turning the ox away, and charging off towards distant hills.

Jae repeats sorrowfully to herself, "I'm making such an effort it's exhausting me, but I'm not getting anywhere. Is that what I deserve?" A few frustrated tears drip silently onto the flattened flowers at her feet.

Waking suddenly and far too early, she has the feeling of having just lost something extremely important.

As the light of a new day begins to illuminate the kitchen, Jae decides this morning she needs to do something completely different. Sipping her hot green tea, she resolves to get out of the house and mingle with other people today, maybe go shopping. As long as you have new shoes and a handbag to match, surely nothing can be wrong with the world?

Leaving her half-empty mug of tea on the table she hurries upstairs to get Chloe ready for school.

Later, she passes a pleasant few hours in a nearby town trying on shoes, searching shops for matching bags, and discovering a couple of colourful scarves. However, her feelings of doubt and longing for something un-nameable return as soon as she finishes. Sipping lukewarm chamomile tea in a café, her purchases in recycled bags at her feet, she texts friends, skim-reads a magazine and stares at passers-by. *Why can't I simply be content like everyone else,* she ruminates finishing the last of her sandwich. *No-one else is as restless and as lost as me. Are they?*

Waiting at the school gates later that afternoon, she spots Chloe intently scanning the crowd of parents for her own mummy. Jae waves and smiles opening her arms to hug the most precious thing in her life. "Hello little darling," she says, thinking how proud and glad she is to be a mother. They walk home slowly, hand-in-hand. But without realising it Jae soon slides into a moody silence. As they reach home Chloe looks questioningly up at her and timidly asks, "what's wrong, mummy?"

With a visceral jolt Jae snaps back to the present, squatting down at her child's eye level and looking at her sincerely. "Nothing's wrong at all, sweetie. I'm sorry," she says hugging her close, "I just think too much! It's a bad habit of mine."

"What are you thinking about?"

"Nothing in particular... I don't really know. Just about life and things... It's a bit silly really. What I really need to be thinking about is what to make you for tea." Her slightly forced jollity does the trick perking them both up. "What do you fancy? Macaroni cheese? Jacket potato? Fish cakes?"

Later that evening after Chloe's in bed, Jae spends some time in her room with Justin. He gives her a half-hearted back-rub while they sip tea, watch TV, and chat a little. Closing her eyes and yielding to the tranquilising effects of the massage, she silently wishes Justin would put a bit more thought into what he is doing. Although it's nice, it could be truly wonderful if he'd only focus more on the task. *How can I hint he's just digging around my shoulders in the same place for too long without sounding bossy and ungrateful? If only he'd move around a bit or concentrate properly it could be so lovely...*

"My turn," Justin says brightly, interrupting her thoughts. Jae suddenly feels cheated of the experience by both her own fault-finding cogitation and Justin's lazy inattention. She sighs, swapping places, and applies herself to giving as good a massage as her fingers allow. "Ah, that's so nice, Jae, thank you…" he murmurs, relaxing thoroughly. His compliment brings an unrestrained smile to her face.

The next morning, waking gradually, Jae flicks the bedroom curtains aside and lies back down again to glare at the top branches of the lifeless magnolia. The sky is leaden grey with hints of blue. Promising, but grey nonetheless. She stays prone on the bed, unmoving, letting the music and words from Beethoven's Mass in C meander persistently through her brain. Her own internal recording that never stops. Then she remembers Chloe's little voice with her innocent yet utterly perceptive question, *"what's wrong mummy?"*

Sighing and turning over onto her side Jae closes her eyes. *I don't know what's wrong. I'm a bit disturbed. I almost feel like I want to give thanks to someone or something, but I've no-one and nothing to give thanks to.*

On her way to the bathroom at little later, she lingers and for the first time properly examines the mundane-looking painting she's hung on the landing opposite her bedroom door. A pastoral scene depicts a man in a straw hat standing next to a cream-coloured bull in a field. They're walking along a barely distinguishable path that winds gently away into the distance. Both bull and man are pictured in profile looking away, so that only the side of their faces are visible. This ingenious perspective invites the viewer to anticipate their journey, or perhaps to follow on behind..?

It's the man from my dream! Jae suddenly knows beyond doubt. *Only, then he was riding a powerful black ox and wasn't wearing a hat.* Curiosity aroused, she peers closer to take in more detail, noting a forbidding sky, thunderous in fact, but with some rays of sunlight illuminating the side of the bull. A storm brews in the near-distance and poppies and daisies cluster at their feet. The creamy-coloured bull points the way ahead with his whole head and body, as if he's on an urgent mission to somewhere important yet obscure. She thinks, *that bull looks the way I feel.*

She notices how the man's arm rests on the back of the bull in a companionable way. They seem to have a silent, shared understanding known only to themselves. The stick in the man's other hand hangs slack, unused. Jae feels a stab of envy for the atmosphere of complicity and collusion between them that excludes her.

Odd. Why did I ever buy this? she asks herself. *I don't really like it as a theme, but, there is something...* The bull is mid-stride, mouth open, momentum propelling him determinedly onward. *I like the purposeful movement in the bull's legs; he's truly on the go. And I like the threat of the dark sky, and the fact that the man seems at one with the bull, almost being led by him, not whipping or coercing him. Two friends out for a walk. If anything the bull is more in charge…*

She realises she's drifted into a sort of trance staring at the painting in her cotton pyjamas, and is now growing cold and desperately needs the loo.

Downstairs she checks her Facebook newsfeed and email deciding to have coffee with her breakfast, instead of the usual mug of tea. Taking a slice of toast back upstairs she shakes her daughter out of sleep, kisses her on the cheek and sits down next to the bed, chewing. "It's time to wake up my darling. School soon!" Receiving no recognisable response from the prone child, she takes a deliberately loud slurp of coffee, continuing in a bright, cheerful voice, "two more days, and then it's the weekend!"

One morning a few days later, with both her parents out at the same time – a rare occurrence – Jae spends time vacuuming the upstairs bedrooms while listening to Radio 4 very loudly on her wireless headphones. Stopping for a light lunch of quiche and green beans, she crouches on the floor against the radiator, her plate balanced on her knees. Questions and thoughts pour into her at every still moment. *What is the point of all this? Who am I? What is truth? Why am I doing this? Is there a God?*

"Maybe I'm lonely," she wonders aloud, getting up and sauntering aimlessly around the house, passing distractedly from room to room. *Too isolated in my life... going a bit mad.* She pauses in the living room gazing at the familiar walls, ornaments, and furniture. *The trouble is, I don't feel particularly lonely, and I love my time at home when everyone's out. So that's not it...*

Absent-mindedly she stares at her reflection in the mirror. She sees an attractive young woman in a red t-shirt, not terribly happy looking, with long, sleek, brown hair and intense hazel eyes. Her reflection does not show a face with a peaceful expression. *My eyes look like they're searching for something. I look worried and anxious.* She slowly executes a smile by degrees until she's grinning like a maniac, but this doesn't make her look less stressed - rather the reverse. Startled, she thinks, *I truly am going mad!*

Feeling a pressing need to go outside and breathe fresh air, she hurriedly pulls on a pair of khaki trainers and heads for the path along the river. Justin is scheduled to collect Chloe from school later this afternoon, and she remembers her parents offered to do the bedtime routine if Jae wanted to stay out late - although she'd declined their offer at the time. At least this means she can take a longer walk now, without having to worry about being back for any particular time.

Outside, the imminent change of season is more evident than usual. It's a few degrees warmer and the air smells fresh and expectant. Jae suddenly wonders whether there are any buds opening on the magnolia tree back at home. She realises, annoyed, that she forgot to check.

Walking quickly with her head down, her red t-shirt shining brightly in the sun, her heart lifts in the spring air while her mind plummets into shadowy, inhospitable caverns. Questions rise up like swords in the dark. What is right, what is wrong? Good, bad? Moral, immoral? What is love? What is death? Does life have a meaning?

Jae grinds her teeth with irritation, *I want to know the meaning, the reason, the purpose. I need to know. I'm worn out from all this thinking, all these unceasing questions...*

In the distance she hears the sound of blackbirds and robins and other excitable spring songbirds. The path seems to have petered out and the grass is thicker and longer at the river's edge. Jae moves distractedly through them, a slight frown of concentration on her face. *I'm searching, searching, pushing through these grasses, but what am I looking for?* Small, frustrated tears swell out from the inner corners of her eyes and disperse on her cheeks. Irritated, she wipes them away with her fingers.

A sudden snort from the adjacent field makes her jump. A cow or bull must be wandering nearby on the other side of the hedge. She hadn't seen it before, so she's surprised and a little unnerved by its loud snuffling and breathing so close at hand. The noise echoes in the still air and seems to follow her as she regains the path. *I hope it's not angry,* she thinks anxiously as she gazes up ahead to see whether the hedge continues. *I don't want to come face-to-face with a big, disgruntled bull.*

Deliberately trying to walk more calmly, a line from the Gloria trickles through her brain. "Gratias agimus tibi propter magnam gloriam tuam" (we give thanks to Thee because of Thy great glory). *I see, hear, and smell your great glory all around me,* she thinks, *but who are You, this supposed creator? Are you chance? God? Mathematics? Nature? I need to sort this out.*

Jae appreciates that the questions are now intruding into her life in such a way that they're starting to negatively affect those around her, most importantly, Chloe. Abruptly deciding she is no longer willing to continue living with these fundamental doubts for single day more, she stops motionless on the path as if halted by a physical impasse.

This is it. I can't go on like this. I'm going to solve this

20

now, today, and I'm not going home until I understand. I owe it to myself, and to Chloe.

There are no more sounds from the bull. Jae walks steadily along singing under her breath, nursing her pact close to her heart, and feeling relieved she's made a decision. The hedge on her left begins to lose its height, opening up the view across the countryside. As Jae glances across the river to a meadow on her right, she notices something incongruous: the field is scattered with tents, stalls, and a large marquee, but without a crowd milling around, or anyone appearing to come or go. *An encampment of tents with no-one entering or leaving? A festival without attendees?*

"Strange," she exclaims aloud, whipping out her mobile phone and looking up 'events', 'celebrations' and 'gatherings' in her area. Nothing.

Not far from where she's standing a small wooden footbridge arches over the river, and on the other side, it seems as if a track leads towards the tented field. The bridge looks ancient although, remarkably, Jae can't remember ever having noticed it before.

She approaches inquisitively before stepping decisively onto the planks, her trainers making little sound as she begins to walk carefully across. Below, the river seems oddly noiseless; a sort of silent, slow-motion sparkling, glimpsed through gaps in the wood beneath her feet.

A muffled hush and stillness descends, like mist, and the further she progresses, the stronger her feelings of unreality become. The only sounds she can hear are her own shallow breathing and the occasional creak of the timber. It's almost as if she's standing on a boat that's gliding soundlessly over the surface of the water without making a ripple. In addition, she has an uncomfortable feeling that this crossing is entirely a one-way journey; that there's no possibility of turning round and going back the way she came. A critical process is being engaged and from this point on, it's forward only.

Stepping off the bridge on the other side of the river, the tension evaporates as the clanking sound of metal repeatedly hitting stone reaches her ears. Pushing open a small wooden gate she passes, greatly intrigued, into the field of tents she'd seen previously, her phone hanging open and forgotten in her hand.

CHAPTER TWO

Spiritual Entertainment

*J*ust inside the entrance to the field, Jae comes across a smallish man wearing a long-sleeved, light green top and casual baggy trousers. He has peculiar untidy brown hair turning grey at the sides, which sticks up like turf on the top of his head. His beard is two-tone: dark around the mouth and moustache, grey everywhere else, and he has a distinctly puzzled expression on his face. He holds a mallet and point chisel half upraised in his hands, and there are cigarette butts scattered in the grass around his feet. Staring in apparent bewilderment at a huge block of white stone directly in front of him, he sighs and puts his head on one side, lowering his tools.

Not wanting to disturb him, Jae stands still off to one side, watching. All of a sudden the man moves rapidly forward and begins to attack one side of the block. Small stone fragments burst from his chisel, sparkling in the sunlight in a frenzy of tapping.

Pausing for a moment he murmurs in a Romanian accent, "what is real is not the appearance, but the idea, the essence of things. There is something pure to be found inside…" and pensively, he mops his brow with a handkerchief taken from his trouser pocket.

Jae answers tentatively, thinking possibly the man was addressing her, "do you mean a precious jewel? Perhaps some gold?"

The man turns to glare at her. "I have no idea," he answers. "I will work at this for months, maybe years. Right now it's just a rough-hewn block of marble. But deep inside something glorious is hidden waiting to be discovered, the essence of the material itself - if only I can lose myself, rid myself of ego, and flow directly into the stone…"

"Oh yes! I understand," replies Jae enthusiastically, "I'm doing the same thing myself."

The man continues to stare at her, and for a moment she thinks she sees approval in his intense grey eyes. "Congratulations. It's a dirty, solitary job, do you not think? With just our simple tools to help us, eh?" he indicates a rasp and tooth chisel laid out on a cloth in the grass. "Every day I will be taking away material, sweating and aching. And yet I'm only uncovering what's already there, hidden from view."

"Exactly!" cries Jae in rapturous agreement, "I'm in the process of doing that too, but in the philosophical sense, in a kind of mental way; I think… no, that didn't come out quite right, what I mean is -" Jae clears her throat noticing the man's attention beginning to wander, "I have some questions about that if you don't mind me asking..?"

But the man shakes his head and turns back to his block of marble, "I'm busy right now. But you could try asking in there." He waves his point chisel toward the tents in the field.

"Oh, okay. Thank you," says Jae a little stung, and leaving the man to glare furiously at the almost imperceptible dent he's made in the rock, she sets off further into the field.

Walking slowly across the grass towards the main marquee, she feels the heat from the sun on her face and arms. Far above, the sky is a vibrant blue with just a few white clouds punching upwards in dramatic thermic action. She hears birds calling excitedly to one another as they soar in the wide azure emptiness. Skylarks, thrushes, blackbirds - all communicating the joy of being alive. *It's a beautiful day*.

Looking ahead, shading her eyes from the glare, she spots a rickety wooden sign banged into the grass indicating the entrance to the marquee. As she approaches, to her astonishment, she sees the words 'Seek and ye shall find' written on it in black paint. With a gasp of astonishment she runs eagerly forward crying, "Vivian! Granny! Are you here? Yes, this is what I want!"

Unnoticed, her mobile phone slips from her fingers and disappears into the grass.

Passing expectantly under the awning and quickly adjusting to the dimmer light, Jae sees a vast indoor area with stalls, tables and seating scattered arbitrarily about. A few people stand or sit on benches and chairs at each booth, but everyone seems to be a stallholder. No guests or visitors, other than herself! There is a low murmur of voices, and the dank green smell of trodden-down grass fills the air. Walking timidly towards the nearest stall, Jae sees a man and woman sitting together on a beautiful curved church pew. As she approaches, they signal for her to join them.

Perching a little uncomfortably on the very edge of the pew, Jae notices a banner above their heads with the words 'Dissolve my heart in floods of tears,' written in black ink.

"Oh how lovely!" she exclaims, relaxing somewhat.

"This is Christianity," says the man, his arms outstretched. He seems to be middle-aged. He has a pleasant, caring expression on his face and speaks in a rich, baritone voice. "The passion of Christ as explained through the devotional music of Bach. The grieving lines of this beautiful aria illustrate how Christians feel about our Saviour the Lord Jesus Christ."

"Oh yes, I know that piece," Jae responds enthusiastically, "it's a soprano solo from the St. John Passion oratorio. Exquisite."

"Those living in Christianity will find further joy of this kind with us." The man and woman look at her steadily, kindly. Jae stares back at them, her mind blank. A suspenseful pause expands between the three of them. Then her heart skips a beat and all at once she knows exactly what to say. "Tell me more," she entreats in a low, urgent tone.

The Christian woman begins to speak gently, her voice calm, yet utterly serious. "Christianity is based on the teachings of Jesus Christ, the Son of God. It offers salvation through his sacrifice on the cross, and eternal life through his resurrection three days later. Jesus proved who he was by his actions when performing miracles and raising the dead, giving us a glimpse of life in his kingdom. This is a place where there is no fear, no suffering, no death," she pauses briefly then continues, emphasising her point perfectly, "imagine the absolute joy of this."

Jae does imagine, and suddenly understands with total clarity, like someone cracking open the lid of a box causing a searing bright light to slice out, how it must feel to believe. So safe, and sure, and comforting.

The woman wrinkles her brow in genuine confusion, "...yet people continue to reject him! This can result in a life of sin: in rejecting Jesus you reject God himself, and are therefore denied a place in the Kingdom of heaven. Jesus called this kind of living, hell: an existence devoid of anything good, forever."

Jae feels thunderstruck and can only stare back at her in helpless silence. The woman gently takes Jae's hand in hers and continues softly, "but don't worry, anyone can be helped by the spirit of the Lord at any time. The doors are **always** open, as long as you genuinely repent and believe. The possibility of living a life of deep security, satisfaction, and happiness is just a leap of faith away."

Letting go of Jae's hand, she turns to her companion who takes over the explanation. He leans in close to Jae, his elbows on his knees. "Apart from our actions in everyday life, our way of communicating with God is through prayer, meditation, and contemplation. Prayer shows you the truth of yourself. It is the practice of faith and hope; a place of humility and the abandonment of pride; the practice of the very Presence of God." He pauses for a moment to let this sink in, and then says, "would you like to experience this with us?"

As they stop talking a tense silence develops, and Jae imagines everyone in the tent must be listening for her answer. She nods, feeling humble, and whispers, "yes."

The man gives her an encouraging smile and says, "I am glad. I will recite a beautiful psalm for you. Listen carefully to these words. Speaking slowly, he begins:

> The Lord is my shepherd;
> I shall not want.
> He maketh me to lie down
> in green pastures:
> He leadeth me beside
> the still waters.
> He restoreth my soul:
> He leadeth me in the paths of
> righteousness for his name's sake.
> Yea, though I walk through the
> valley of the shadow of death,
> I will fear no evil:
> For thou art with me;
> Thy rod and thy staff they comfort me.
> Thou preparest a table before me in
> the presence of mine enemies:
> Thou anointest my head with oil;
> my cup runneth over.
> Surely goodness and mercy shall
> follow me all the days of my life:
> And I will dwell in the
> house of the Lord forever."

As he orates Jae experiences something profound

and spiritual shift inside her soul. The words are beautiful, meaningful. They bring to life a place and a way of being that's deeply comforting, pleasant, and affirming. It describes a wonderful, loving, and inclusive vision of a person safe and cherished in life; someone who can even walk close to death without fear; someone who is completely confident of the protecting love of their God. The words are the very embodiment of goodness, beauty, and love. Standing up slowly, she says in a solemn voice, "thank you. That was genuinely moving, and beautiful. Let me think about it. Give me a moment…"

Standing motionless next to the pew for a while, Jae stares into space letting the words seep in more deeply, and allowing her thoughts to compose themselves.

Coming back into focus she realises she's walked a few paces away from the Christians. Without consciously noticing, she's turned towards another stall nearby, which now immediately catches her attention. A different couple sit together on a mat on the floor. The man has a short, neatly trimmed beard, the woman a headscarf. On the banner above them are written the words, 'The First and the Last, and the Outward and the Inward.'

"Oh!" cries Jae to herself, "I must talk to the others too." She thanks the Christians for all that they've given her, waves goodbye, and turns and steps forward to greet the friendly-looking couple on the floor.

"Please sit with us," the woman smiles, indicating a spot on the thickly woven mat. Jae sits down cross-legged, smiling back, and simply says, "tell me."

Looking directly at Jae, and in a serious, almost

austere voice, the man bluntly asks, "why am I a Muslim?"

This isn't what Jae is expecting. She opens her mouth to reply, takes a deep breath, but can't immediately formulate an answer. "Um…" she feels as if she really should address the question properly, then realises she hasn't a clue why this particular man might believe in Islam.

"Er," her thoughts race, "hmmm. Is it because you were born into the religion? Your parents are Muslim, so you are too..?" This feels a bit feeble but it's all she can think of on the spot.

"That may be factually correct," answers the man with a friendly chuckle, "but that's not the reason I'm a Muslim. No, the reason, quite simply, is because Islam is the truth." He pauses to sip some water before continuing agreeably, "Islam completely satisfies me as a human being. Firstly and essentially it's given me personal experience of communing with God. Actually I have no need of any other reason for believing than this one pure fact. However I am also completely convinced by the detailed explanations of Islam's decrees, laws, and doctrines – the evidence of which can easily be found in the Quran – the book of the word of God."

He continues, "Islam is reasonable; it satisfies my intellect; it helps to control my human desires, elevating them to a higher moral plane, and it gives me everything I need as a guide to life. In my religion I find peace and comfort, instruction and explanation, but above all it enables me to establish a close personal bond between myself and my maker."

The woman now takes over, "the Holy Prophet Muhammad, peace be upon him, was the last of the many prophets, including Isaac, Moses, David, and Jesus - and others - that God sent to earth to relay his divine message. Islam is therefore the most recent and perfect description of God's will. The word "Islam" itself basically means 'peace,' 'purity,' 'submission' and 'obedience.' All of that. We, who follow Islam, are first and foremost obedient to Allah, but we also try to establish peace in our lives, and a relationship of tolerance and equality with all his creations. We believe that every child is born completely sinless into this world, and it is only when a person consciously and deliberately breaks the laws of Allah that he can be called a sinner."

There is a brief silence while Jae absorbs all she's heard, before the woman continues, "in preparation for prayer we perform Wudhu to ensure we're properly cleaned and purified before we speak to God. Without this, our prayers are not accepted."

With those words the man and woman get up gracefully and disappear into the interior of the stall behind them. Jae waits, listening to the sound of water splashing on marble, and when they emerge she sees they've taken off their shoes. The man walks to the very edge of the prayer mat and faces a south-easterly direction. The woman stands facing the same way a little behind him. Jae positions herself off the prayer mat on the grass over to one side. She wants to catch every word they utter without intruding on their space. After a short pause the man raises his hands to either side of his face and solemnly declares, "Allahu akbar." His hands then fall to his chest where he gently clasps them. The woman follows his movements precisely. Continuing, the man speaks in English with a soft Arabic accent:

"Pure from imperfection are you,
Allah The glory is Yours
Blessed is Your Name
Your Majesty is most high
there is no God but You."

Jae closes her eyes and allows the words to enter her being. A truly beautiful sound; it has a calming, quietening effect on her soul.

"In the name of Allah,
the Beneficent, the Merciful
The glory belongs to Allah,
the Lord of all worlds,
The beneficent, the Merciful
Ruler of the Day of Judgement.
You alone do we worship and You
alone do we ask for help.
Guide us to the straight path,
The path of those upon whom You
have bestowed Your favours,
Not of those upon whom is
Your wrath, nor the astray."

Another verse trickles through Jae's consciousness and then, as she opens her eyes, the Muslims in front of her bow forward together in unison, hands on knees, still standing.

"God is the greatest.
Glory be to my Lord Almighty."

They stand upright once more, their arms hanging loosely by their sides and mutter, "God listens to those who praise Him. Our Lord, praise be to you."

And then in one fluid, graceful movement they both fall to their knees, palms pressed to the ground, head still a little upraised, saying, "God is the Greatest."

Jae stands up startled. Their prayer is so passionate and heartfelt! She realises she is witnessing a true communion between two people and their God. Nothing can disturb them or come between them. She watches as their heads gently come into contact with the floor, their trembling voices lowered. "Glory be to my Lord, the Most High."

As Jae backs slowly away they kneel up, eyes closed, heads facing down towards the floor, and continue speaking fervently, "God is the greatest. My God forgive me, forgive me…"

She moves further away and their voices become a quiet murmur as, once more, they place their heads directly on the mat, "God is the Greatest…."

Such piety, deference, and passion! What security and satisfying humility it must create when you truly believe in Islam. How enticing… Jae feels she can truly appreciate why someone would be drawn to this religion. It provides the opportunity to become part of a global family, embraced by a people who share a common sense of togetherness through deep understanding, and a core love of the one God. It must give you a wonderful sense of belonging…

Moving a little distance away from the praying couple, watching their devotion in something of an intellectual daze, she thinks about what they've said and how it compares with the Christian couple she was talking to previously. She can't say that they are dramatically unalike in feel and aim, or that one is better or more obvious that the other – it's just the words, actions, and some of the content that's different. It's a strange and unexpected discovery…

Suddenly, her thoughts are interrupted by the clear chime of a bell or gong. Turning round she sees a third stall, in front of which, on a low wooden platform, sit two people with shaved heads wearing orange robes. A banner hangs above them proclaiming, 'Find out for yourself what is truth, what is real.'

Rushing forward, she cries out, "yes, that's it! I am! I'm trying so hard… but all I'm doing is entangling myself further in the thickets."

The seated woman has just stuck a bronze gong suspended from a small, gilded, black lacquered stand. It releases an arrestingly beautiful sound of complete purity.

"Hello. Hello, Buddhists!" Jae proclaims in a loud, ecstatic voice.

The woman looks at her and smiles slowly, gesturing to the gong with her eyes. Jae had thought it ceased making a noise several seconds ago, but becoming silent, she now realises it's still sounding sweetly and delicately into the air. The three of them remain unmoving for a while, concentrating quietly together, allowing the sound of the bell to become fainter and fainter until they can truly hear it no more.

After a pause, Jae apologises feeling clumsy and brash. "I'm sorry, I thought the gong had already stopped ringing. I didn't realise it would continue sounding for so long."

"No problem." With their shaved heads and identical saffron-coloured robes it's not immediately easy to determine which is male and which female, if indeed they are of different genders. The Buddhist continues, "we're used to listening attentively to all the sounds of life beyond the time when others think they can hear nothing at all."

Jae suddenly becomes aware that her mobile phone hasn't rung for ages, nor has it bleeped a text or e-mail alert. She also realises that she hasn't checked it recently, nor wanted to. In a reflex movement her hands seek the reassuring shape in her pockets, but it isn't there. Instead of a rush of anxiety, she finds, at this moment in time, she doesn't much care - which is pretty unusual. She also realises she very much wants to speak to the Buddhists.

Just then her attention is caught by three monks on the left of the platform. Leaning over the floor, their faces a few inches from the wood, they've just finished creating a most magnificent, colourful and intricately detailed, sand mandala.

"Why that's stunning!" exclaims Jae, leaning forward for a closer inspection. "That's just fantastically beautiful. Amazing! I'm sorry I just need to get my phone…" Jae urgently pats her pockets again, while staring in awe at the work of art before her. If she could just take a photo or two, or maybe a video, she could upload it to Facebook and show everyone how amazing the Buddhists' artwork is.

As she digs in the front and back pockets of her shorts, she sees that what has been created on the floor is an enormous vibrant circle, decorated inside with intricate designs and patterns enclosing several even more elaborate-looking bands. Some have foreign writing in them, some are a plain single colour, and others filled with many-coloured swirls and flower-like designs. Towards the middle, a huge square containing dozens of other squares gives a 3D effect as her gaze is drawn in to the very centre of the picture – an almost indiscernible flower pattern within squares within squares. Jae doesn't know where to look next; it's so rich and detailed. Decorating the rings and layers are various animals depicted in brilliant colours: deer, snakes, horses and elephants - a magnificently interwoven meaningful depiction of everything that is Buddhist. She can pick out images of the wheel of life, the eternal knot, and banner - all incorporated into the picture at every edge and in many of the large outer squares. And the most astonishing thing of all, is that the whole achievement is fashioned entirely from millions of grains of brightly dyed sand.

Sensing an audience, the monks look up from their work of slowly flowing sand through hand-held metal funnels. This picture looks as though it must have taken weeks of intense concentrated effort in an act of great love and meditation.

Jae is distracted by being unable to find her phone, but out of the corner of her eye notices one of the monks get up, stretch, and study the completed work of art for a moment. The other monks then sit back contentedly, while the first monk takes a broom from the side of the platform and advances towards the sand painting.

"Oh no! Stop! No, please, wait," Jae cries rushing forward holding out her hands, "please don't sweep it away; it would be such a great pity, such a waste of effort…"

But it's too late. The broom sweeps a purposeful wide streak through the very centre of the highly ordered design. Sand grains swirl together into ugly chaos, forming a gaudy mess of indeterminate shape. The monks proceed to sweep it ceremoniously off the platform and onto the grass, where it just disappears from view as if it never existed.

Aghast, Jae turns towards the sitting monk and nun. "Why did they do that?" she demands to know.

The two Buddhists regard her steadily, allowing a space to form in the air between them after her question, leaving her to listen alone to her racing, directionless thoughts. Calming down and taking a few deep breaths she sits down heavily on the bare floorboards opposite the two Buddhists. She sighs and asks again, this time more calmly, "why did they destroy that beautiful picture?"

It's the man who answers in a gentle voice, "we destroy the mandala as a reminder that we are all impermanent. Nothing is forever. No state, whether good or bad, is permanent. As human beings, it is our mistaken belief that things last, and this is a central cause of suffering. We must come to know deep in the core of our beings, that we too, one day, will be destroyed just as easily and as quickly as erasing a mandala. In this way it teaches the precept of non-attachment."

"But, isn't that a bit depressing?" asks Jae, alarmed and feeling a little frightened.

"Not at all," answers the woman, "whatever arises, ceases. It's simply the Wheel of Life. As selfish human beings we're trapped in this cycle of birth, suffering, death and re-birth. Our goal is to escape from all this, achieving total liberation from the craving that leads to greed, hatred, violence and confusion. We attempt this through the Four Noble Truths."

Jae's interest is deeply sparked. "What are the Four Noble Truths?"

"They are the four steps to enlightenment," the nun smiles kindly in response. "Firstly, the knowledge that life is suffering. Secondly, that the origin of suffering is craving. Thirdly, that the cessation of suffering is nirvana - that profound peace of mind achieved with total liberation; and fourthly, the noble eightfold path is the gateway to the cessation of suffering."

"Ahh," murmurs Jae reverently, rolling the phrase around on her tongue, "the noble eightfold path. This all sounds very intriguing."

"Yes," says the monk, "it's the entry into awakening. You must cultivate and realise complete view, thought, speech, action, livelihood, effort, mindfulness, and concentration. Through the noble eightfold path one gains a rare life, not driven by narcissistic craving and attachment. A person who has achieved enlightenment, truly and fully, embraces the Three Jewels."

"The Three Jewels!" Jae repeats, mesmerised, her mind overrun with exotic images from far-off lands in ancient times. She's starting to feel the warm, fuzzy floating feeling she once experienced after swallowing a pre-med pill prior to an operation. Just the words of Buddhism intoxicate her. *The three jewels...*

At this moment, however, Jae's realises her legs are starting to get pins-and-needles; and although the Buddhists are sitting perfectly still without fidgeting or shuffling, she feels a strong urge to straighten out to avoid the rapid onset of cramp. Staring at them, sitting unmoving in the same position, she wonders how they can possibly sit there in such an uncomfortable state for so long, and on a hard wooden platform too. Unable to sit still any longer, she suddenly bursts out, "I'm sorry, my legs are killing me!"

The Buddhists chuckle. "Just stand or move about whenever you wish. Don't force yourself to sit in a painful position or do anything you don't want to do."

Jae stands with great relief, leaning on one leg, stretching out the other, and feeling the blood return and the pain recede.

"You can stay standing for puja if you like," the nun offers.

"Oh yes please, that would be great," replies Jae as the Buddhists stand up and begin organising a little statue, a small bunch of flowers and some candles and incense, which they light with matches. A beautiful smell rises into the air around them. Sitting facing the newly created shrine, feet pointing away from the image of the Buddha, they begin to softly chant.

> "Through the working of Great
> Compassion in their hearts,
> May all beings have happiness
> and the causes of happiness;
> May all be free from sorrow
> and the causes of sorrow;
> May all never be separated from the
> sacred happiness, which is sorrowless;
> And may all live in equanimity
> Without too much attachment
> and too much aversion,
> and live believing in the equality of
> all that lives. Namo Amida Buddha."

A great stillness and silence envelops the marquee.

Again Jae gets the impression that everyone in the tent has ceased their activities to listen and watch her reaction. The Buddhists sit perfectly still, peaceful; heads bowed, eyes closed, unaffected by any audience.

The words of their reflection arouse a wave of emotion in her, almost a love for them and their humble and beautiful wishes. To be in the presence of great and genuine selflessness, to hear true desire to help all beings, without condition, is deeply moving. Jae feels as if she's being loved by the Buddhists, by the very words of their prayer, and in turn she loves them back.

However, she's not sure about the idea that this precious life she has now is beyond salvation - that it needs to be renounced and overcome in order to reach an exclusive state of awakening not easily attainable to ordinary people. Beautiful though it undoubtedly is, pure and good though its motivations obviously are, it's still a belief-based thought system, and in this way not greatly different from Christianity or Islam, nor indeed any other religion.

Looking around the tent, her eyes come to rest on a previously unnoticed door flap leading out of the marquee. She can see bright spring sunlight in the field beyond, and in a sudden desire to be in the open-air, she bows sincerely to the Buddhists and takes her leave in silence.

Outside it feels glorious to breathe fresh air and feel the sun on her skin again. Sitting down in the grass on a small knoll, she reflects on her experiences with the three religions.

Each one is centred around an authoritative and

intelligent leader. Each is based on ancient texts written and collated hundreds of years ago, describing the ethical and daily-life practices and doctrines of the time. They each claim to present unique pathways to true wisdom and a good, compassionate life - along with many possible punishments if one chooses not to adhere to the recommended strictures. Each is quite beautiful in its own way but with surprisingly similar ethical values, methods of devotion, and meditation. Each religion also offers some form of transcendence of the self.

In the end, does it really matter which religion I choose? Jae wonders, *aren't they all just offering the same thing in a different language?*

It seems to Jae that religion presents a profound and sustaining support for people in need of a divine belief, for those who require a way of living that's highly organised and easy to define. Practised sincerely, it appears to give people genuine moments of their own vanishing, as she has discovered witnessing the Christians, Moslems, and Buddhists in moments of devotion. The limited contact they have with something greater than themselves - that silent sacred space they find during prayer and through acts of worship - provides just enough spirituality for people to be satisfied that they have their answer. However, simply carrying on like that day by day, prevents them from being able to confront any of the other, more profound issues of illusion and deceit revealed through deeper examination. They may see to the core of things very briefly, Jae muses, but does it take them beyond that first little step? Do they ever venture out of their pre-defined ways of thinking into that which lies beyond?

She allows her mind to settle of its own accord, becoming calmer, like the fading ripples on the surface of a pond after a disturbance. Although superficially different, each religion seems to offer a similar guarantee: spiritual healing in a world devoid of holy experience, a belief for people to dive into and immerse themselves in. Religion gives people something to hold on to, somewhere to hide - a place of private meaning and purpose. Jae feels that it's simply a matter of having faith and personal conviction in something: all you have to do is believe, and the plausible arguments will fall into place, whichever religion you plump for.

Any religion can give me meaning, Jae silently concludes, *a route to belonging, a group in which I'll feel safe, respected, protected and loved. But I don't need that! I already have a family. I don't need a religion to provide me with security. I'm looking for my meaning in the wrong place.* Closing her eyes tight shut, she thinks, *where then, if not religion?*

Opening her eyes and scanning the field, she spots a group of people standing casually together under a tree not far away. Getting up she decides to join them, and as she arrives, they greet her cordially.

"Hello," says one of the men. "I think you could be looking for us."

Jae smiles in agreement, "yes, I think I could."

"Very good," a young woman nods, congratulating Jae. Everyone in the group is dressed casually in jeans, tops and jackets, and they all appear to be quite young, ranging from mid-twenties to not much older than herself.

"Why thank you," Jae replies, feeling pleased with herself.

A man in a pink shirt with rolled-up sleeves indicates the others one by one. "This is Simon, Polly, Mary, and Evan," he explains, "we're all brothers and sisters. And I'm Jim."

"You're siblings?" Jae asks raising her eyebrows.

"Yes, literally… and also non-literally."

"What do you mean?"

Polly explains. "Humanists find meaning and joy in life just as it is, treating everyone equally regardless of age, gender, skin colour, sexual orientation, religious belief, or any other factor that differentiates one from another. A person is a person and all are of equal value in our eyes: why should I treat you any differently from my own sister?"

"I suppose that's the ideal…" begins Jae, "but is that not very similar to Buddhism?"

"In a way yes," answers Mary, a short lady with a sleek blonde bob, "but the vital difference is that Humanist thinking has no supernatural, ascetic, or metaphysical underpinning. Our core values are rooted in reason, compassion, democracy, human rights, the rule of law, and so on. We live ethical, secular lives and think for ourselves about what's right or wrong, moral or immoral. Living a full and happy life is accessible to people from every level of society, not just the elite few who undergo a certain number of pilgrimages or recite a particular number of prayers. We don't require an external authority to give us one-size-fits-all rules." The speaker is earnest, gesticulating gently with her hands.

"Yes I understand," acknowledges Jae.

Mary continues, "everything we need is within

43

each of us already, having been repeatedly demonstrated to us via our parents when we were children, and by friends and colleagues as we matured. The proof of this lies in understanding why we're all not just horrible to everyone all the time."

Jae smiles.

"I mean," Mary continues, "why aren't we? We might do pretty well by being a truly nasty person! But generally, no-one wants to live that way; we feel it's wrong. We want to be pleasant, nice, get along with people. But why?"

"Yes why?" Jae asks, fascinated, genuinely wanting to know the answer.

Evan, an attractive young man with a shock of thick, dark hair, takes up the thread, "because it's natural. You see, for us, there's no need for a belief in a God to make us behave well or live a generous and intelligent life. Recognising the dignity of every individual, celebrating human achievement and potential, acknowledging progress… it's all for its own sake. Just as it is. There's no grand scheme, no 'creator' overseeing things. We look to science for explanations of the big life question."

Jae waves a fly away from her head. "So when we misbehave or act immorally it's just due to a lack of intelligence, education, or understanding?"

"Exactly so. As our friends the Buddhists might say, 'there is no sin, only ignorance.' We live lives with rooted values that aren't attributed to God figures or ancient fantastical stories, but come simply from within our own selves."

A thoughtful silence develops and Jae feels this is the nearest to an idea or philosophy she's encountered so far that could potentially fulfil her.

But she still worries that it isn't quite getting to the core of things, as if it's almost there, but just missing the point. Humanists may have found a significant emptiness, but they seem to go no further. It all just stops there, with the individual, with people.

"Is this the best we can do?" she asks, "is that it? Just people, people, people?"

"What more could you want?" asks Simon with a smile and a shrug.

But humanism is still a belief, thinks Jae, still a sort of home for people who need a home. A group to belong to. How is that different from religion? And how does this fit with the fact that essentially we are completely and utterly alone? Is there not a way of being complete as an individual, without belonging to anything?

She starts to speak slowly, working it out as she goes along. "I see the nothingness you point to; it's attractive, simple, harmless, but somehow, if you'll forgive me, it seems a bit shallow. I think you could go further…"

Suddenly a loud cry of irritation interrupts her comments, and turning hastily round she sees two or three people seated at a table some distance off, gesticulating wildly and shouting at each other.

Turning back to the family group, she says, "Jim, Mary, everyone. I do see what you're saying, and I don't disagree. In fact I think it's completely honourable. However, I still feel Humanism is missing something vital, or rather, not developing its concept far enough…"

"You're hard to please!" laughs Simon.

"I know that," smiles Jae ruefully. "Please excuse me, I think I have somewhere else to go now."

The Humanists wave her off, friendly and accepting, as she somewhat regretfully turns to walk the short distance through the grass towards the small group of shouting men. This is proving to be one of the most interesting, if perplexing, days of her life. Gratitude and excitement froth wildly through her veins, and she skips a few steps out of pure delight. *Today I am living spring!* she thinks, giggling quietly to herself.

Approaching what appears to be a games table, she immediately recognises a backgammon board with checkers mid-game, and sees a nine point match on the go.

An intense-looking man standing near the table studying the board looks up as she joins them. "Fancy a drink? Or maybe a mushroom?" He has a German accent and a pretty magnificent moustache, which Jae suppresses the urge to stroke.

"A mushroom?? No, no thank you. But some water would be lovely," she responds.

Moustache Man indicates a cold-looking glass of water at the edge of the table nearest her. Drinking deeply and feeling greatly refreshed, she leans toward the board to study the positions. "I love backgammon," she says, in a lowered, conspiratorial voice.

The score is eight-six to black on the Crawford, which prohibits the use of the doubling cube essentially making this particular game a one-pointer - a game with a far greater chance of chance itself deciding the outcome.

Mr Moustache yawns deeply, seemingly in response to her comment making Jae feel a little put out. He appears to notice. "I'm sorry", he says in a friendly manner, "I don't sleep very well these days; I'm always tired."

"And ill," shouts one of the players seated at the table, who also seems to be of German origin. "Fred's usually got one thing or another wrong with him. If he isn't complaining of stomach-ache or indigestion, he's got a dreadful migraine or a stabbing pain in his side. Worst of all, sometimes he thinks he's Polish."

"Yes, thank you, Martin," replies Fred taking a long gulp from a glass of red wine, "you yourself have a heart condition worse than any of my complaints, so I advise you to maintain concentration. Your winning streak could change at any moment."

"Whose go is it?" asks Jae

"Well as everyone knows, Martin has just completed his turn, so it must be John's," Fred says.

"Ssshh," Martin's opponent across the table suddenly hisses at them in a French accent. "I'm about to roll."

Everyone looks to the board. Dressed rather smartly in a suit, and wearing glasses, John picks up the red precision dice, pops them into his shaker and makes a big deal of rattling them around. He looks up smirking.

"Oh Lord," Fred coughs into his hand. "John, if you don't act now I'm going to have to declare you dead, and as you very well know God is already dead, so you're going nowhere fast."

"I know God is dead – that's obvious," John scoffs in reply, "but I also know that at the same time my whole being continuously cries out for God." He stops shaking the dice and stares at Fred. "There's no need to worry about me **acting**, it's my profound concern."

"It's not what you **do** that matters," interjects Martin, "but **what** and **how** and **that** you know you are acting, whenever you eventually get round to it."

Jae doesn't completely understand what Martin has just pronounced, but feels a kind of kinship with John. "So you're saying that you desperately want something that you know doesn't exist..? Well this is exactly what's bothering me!"

"Count on no-one but yourself young lady," John glowers from his chair. "We are our choices; you are your life – and nothing else."

"Yes, I see that," Jae answers, "I know. And I know I am alone in this."

"Nothingness is something very positive," Martin declares.

"That's one of the most intelligible things you've ever said," Fred cries, throwing his hands into the air. "Usually no-one can make head nor tail of anything you say. Now, John, **roll the dice!**"

John rolls and everyone bends forward to see the numbers. When the dice stop moving they show a one and a six.

"One-six!" they shout in unison. This miraculous and shocking roll turns the match completely around from an almost certain loss for John, to an almost certain win. John's checker leaps off the bar hitting Martin's blot on the one-point, putting that checker itself on the bar; and with the six, John escapes the five-point prime Martin had lined up against him.

Martin laughs uproariously. "It's the ladder on square number eighty!"

Fred joins in the amusement, but John seems to accept the roll as if it's nothing unexpected.

"What a joker!" exclaims Martin. "John, only you

could go from being hopelessly lost, to favourite-to-win with a ridiculous lover's leap like that."

"More like love a sleep," remarks Fred still laughing. "You barely have to be awake to make such a move. It's pretty forced. You have no choice but to come off the bar and therefore hit, and who wouldn't also jump the prime?"

John says, "it's absurd, and perfectly normal. I accept it completely."

Looking up at Jae, John suddenly remarks in a mischievous tone, "it's utterly terrifying is it not? The burden we all bear of complete responsibility for our actions amidst an absurd world where anything can happen to anyone, at any time… It's enough to drive a man insane. Look at Fred," and he points rudely at his companion.

Jae turns to look at Fred standing off to one side rolling his eyes to the sky, muttering something in Hebrew about Dionysus the Greek God of wine. All at once, he comes back into the present and taking Jae firmly by the arm, looks at her directly, "if you wish to strive for peace of soul and pleasure, then believe; if you wish to be a devotee of truth, then inquire."

Jae feels a rush of love for this friendly, eccentric, moustachioed man. What he says strikes a deep chord. "Yes, yes, I am of the same mind."

From behind them at the table John suddenly announces: "The next roll of the dice will decide whether Jae lives or dies." And picking up shaker, he starts rattling the dice around noisily as if about to roll.

"No, NO! I don't agree," shouts Jae, a little frightened. "This is not for me."

"Oh but it is, my dear. Every decision you make defines you," Martin reminds Jae. "Your way of questioning expresses your very nature. There is absolutely nothing else. To prove it, we will make the dice the decision-maker. If they give us a double, you live, any other roll, you die by suicide."

"No, please don't!" Jae implores, starting to feel genuinely frightened, "I reject this way of living."

"Not so fast," says John. "Why **not** let your ontological crisis be decided by the outcome of the next dice roll? Why not relinquish all your worries and questions about how to live, in favour of the ultimate freedom of making decisions according to pure luck? It's the definitive statement of meaninglessness: you have complete freedom to live your life without any control, including your own!"

This stops Jae in her tracks. She thinks rapidly, *am I a gambler? Do I believe I have complete responsibility of my every action? Why, yes I do. Do I reject an overriding divine power or designer? Yes, I do. Do I accept emptiness? Certainly. But do I accept that emptiness is completely meaningless? No, no I do not.*

Jae realises the three men are motionless and staring at her, waiting for her response. "No," she finally says out loud, "no I don't agree. I'm leaving now. But thank you…"

And without waiting to see whether John rolls the dice or what the numbers might be, she abruptly turns and runs away from the table and the three arguing Europeans.

Hastening deeper into the field towards what looks like a little summer house, she feels in desperate need of some rest. Ideally, she would like to discuss her thoughts and experiences, and all that she's been going through, with a sympathetic listener. "I need a bit of 'me' time," she says out loud.

Breathing quickly, and with a thumping heart, she approaches the summer house only to see it's more of a folly or miniature temple than an actual house or pavilion. Built in Greco-Roman style it has two plain Doric columns at the front, supporting a typical, moderately decorative pyramid-shaped roof. Pushing open an ancient-looking wooden door positioned between the two columns, Jae passes through what appears to be an enormous picture frame into a comfortable-looking, if somewhat gloomy, study. It feels like walking into a museum. There are several photographs and paintings adorning the walls, notably one directly opposite the entrance, of an enormous beautifully constructed bridge over a ravine. Closing the door behind her, Jae sees various ornaments and interesting-looking objects and antiquities cluttered together on shelves and little tables scattered around the room. She notices an overcoat flung over a chair, a walking stick leaning up against the wall, a glass display cabinet stuffed from top to bottom with various bottles and vases, and an extremely inviting-looking chaise-longue with cushions and blankets, pushed up against the far wall. A large oriental rug decorated with colourful geometric shapes covers the floor, and any extra space seems to have been taken up with bookshelves crammed with hard-backed, leather-bound, serious-looking tomes.

An older gentleman sits at a desk off to one side scribbling notes on a pad of paper. He sports a close-cropped grey beard and smokes a large cigar. The room smells fusty and smoky, but not off-puttingly so. Strangely comforting. Grandfatherly.

As Jae collapses onto the chaise and pulls a blanket up to her chest, her eyes come to rest on something unpleasant: a preserved, stuffed bull's head mounted on a wooden shield on the opposite wall next to the door.

"Oh, excuse me that's disgusting," she blurts out, sitting up twisting uncomfortably to avert her eyes. "I don't think I can lie here and stare at that!"

"Oh dear," the bearded gentleman responds congenially. "Please don't concern yourself, it's a problem easily solved." He stands up and walks across the room to un-hook the shield from the wall. Staggering with his unwieldy burden to a far corner of the study, he places the stuffed head carefully on the floor out of sight.

"Thank you, that's very kind," Jae replies gratefully." I just find it a little disturbing…" Her voice trails off as she relaxes back on the chaise and tries to formulate why. "I recently had a dream about a beautiful ox walking along a path through a meadow. A man wearing a large straw hat was there as his companion, and although he had a whip in his hand, he didn't use it. It was a lovely dream."

She pauses in thought for a moment, "or actually, was it a dream? Maybe I was there myself – yes, that's it! I saw them together in a field by the river on my way here. Although now I'm trying to recall it, I really can't be sure… I do know that the bull and the man were happy companions travelling off somewhere together, and I felt very much like I wanted to join them."

"Yes," agrees the therapist, "a very interesting

dream indeed." Jae imagines she sees a glint in his eyes, but he continues brusquely, "we have an hour together now, and we will talk about whatever you wish. Anything at all. However, I must first tell you that our session here will cost you fifty pounds."

"Fifty pounds?!" she sits up again abruptly, anxiety spiking. "I'm sorry I don't have that kind of money on me." Standing up she pats her pockets wondering how to leave without it being too embarrassing. Suddenly her hands feel a lump in the back pocket of her shorts, and pulling it out she finds a small bundle of notes. Unfolding the money it's exactly fifty pounds.

"But how on earth did that get there?" she asks, staring in astonishment at the money.

Before she can query it any more, or put it back in her pocket and run, the psychoanalyst thanks her and indicates a wooden box on a little hexagonal coffee table next to the chaise lounge.

"Um… well…" Jae stutters, and without knowing quite why, drops the money into the receptacle and subsides slowly back onto the chaise.

A silence mists into the room. Jae wraps the blankets around her, lies back and stares moodily at the ceiling. *That was fifty quid!* Her thoughts race, imagining everything she could have spent it on.

The therapist is out of her line of sight now that she's lying properly on the chaise, and Jae wonders how she might start speaking again to break the uncomfortable atmosphere that now exists. However he relieves her of the trouble by suddenly stating in a business-like manner, "before I can say anything to you I must know a great deal about you; please tell me what you know about yourself."

Jae takes a deep breath, but then only sighs. Where to begin?

The therapist continues, "one more thing before you start. What you tell me must differ in one respect to ordinary conversation. Instead of trying to keep a connecting thread running through your remarks, in this room you should include any side-issues, intrusive ideas, or irrelevancies you would normally omit. You need to say whatever goes through your mind. Act as though, for instance, you were a traveller sitting next to a window of a railway carriage describing to someone inside the carriage the changing views which you see on the outside. Finally, never forget that you have promised to be honest, and never leave anything out because for some reason or another it is unpleasant to tell."

"Well... okay then. But I don't think I have anything particularly unpleasant to relate," Jae replies hesitantly, "it's just that... I've been plagued with persistent questions and thoughts lately. For several months in fact. Philosophical thoughts about the meaning of my life, and of life in general. I spend far too long every day wondering what 'The Truth' is, if indeed there is such a thing as the truth. It's really taking over my life, causing problems between my family and me. I seem to ask myself what the point of it all is every other moment. I wonder if there's something else, something 'other'... some spiritual meaning to find or attain, like Buddhist enlightenment, religious faith, or philosophical revelation. I feel like I need some kind of spiritual dimension in my life because this is what's lacking, I think."

"Mmm." The therapist scribbles in his notepad.

"I know that probably means I'm neurotic, but I think everybody must be neurotic to some degree – including you. Especially you," and then thinking she may have been a bit blunt, hastily adds, "I'm sorry, but you did say to include **every** thought."

The psychotherapist makes no comment at this last remark, and after a little pause, Jae continues her free association: "I feel like I've started on a quest, a journey of metaphysical discovery to find something I've lost, or a place of being that I've no idea about yet; but that I could attain under the right conditions, and thereafter live a fulfilled and peaceful life.."

Even to Jae this sounds confused and fanciful. The therapist still says nothing, preferring instead to concentrate on his notepad and whatever it is he's writing there.

"Um, and it's a desperate need," she perseveres, "a pressing distraction from my daily life. It bothers me all the time. As I said, I think about these issues almost every waking moment and it's starting to make me feel slightly unhinged." Jae laughs self-consciously, "obviously I'm in the right place for that!"

A cavernous silence swallows her last sentence, and she fidgets nervously with the fringed edge of her blanket. The fact that the therapist doesn't say a word somehow compels Jae to keep speaking. It feels like a trick, but she doesn't resist. She needs to talk.

She sighs, and after a while continues in a serious almost reverential voice, "I need to find the answers, and I feel exhausted and depleted by the efforts I'm making."

As she finishes, her eyes focus on a heavy baroque mirror on the opposite wall, positioned exactly where she could have sworn the bull head was hanging before the therapist removed it. Staring up at it, she thinks she hears, or rather actually sees, music emerging from it in a kind of psychedelic vapour. It's the slow, soothing Dona Nobis Pacem from the end of Beethoven's Agnus Dei for his Mass in C. And as she watches and listens, Jae feels her eyes slowly close of their own accord and her body become weightless and completely relaxed as an exhausted stupor overcomes her.

Opening her eyes a few minutes later (or is it hours?) she blinks up at the mirror. There's no music now, just the steady rhythm of hypnotic ticking coming from a clock on the desk.

From her prone position on the couch she can see reflected only a dark corner of the ceiling, prompting her to think that no matter how long she lies here talking about herself, she's not going to get any further along the path towards her goal - whatever that is.

She sits up and stretches, then turns to face the psychotherapist. "I'm sorry, I don't think this is quite the right place for me. I'm on an intellectual quest, but even so; I don't think the answer lies here within my own brain, within the repetitive, mechanical action of my thoughts. My mind can't examine itself. It's not that clever."

Surprised, the therapist puts down his pen and looks up from his papers. Jae is standing now, refreshed and reinvigorated, a determined expression on her face. She's cast the blanket aside and it lies crumpled and rejected on the chaise.

"You may find that outside of your own brain there is only a vast emptiness," he says gravely, studying her closely.

"I'm willing to take that chance."

They stare at each other in charged silence for a few moments, which he eventually breaks with, "well then, you are free to go. I wish you all the sexcess in the world."

Wondering whether he actually said it or she heard it wrong, Jae steps through the frame-door and out into the vestibule of the temple.

Nothing worth worshipping in there, she thinks with a toss of her head, and walks briskly away into the sunshine.

The further she walks, the better she feels; and reaching the edge of the field she comes across a group of people sitting round a large rectangular table under the gigantic boughs of a magnificent mature beech tree.

I do believe I'm getting somewhere, she thinks, feeling optimistic and resolute.

"What a majestic old tree," she remarks out loud as she passes under its shady sphere.

"Yes, it's truly glorious," somebody answers. There are several people sharing some lunch together – bread, cheese, eggs, salad, cold meat.

"Take a pew," invites someone else, inciting a few sniggers from the others. As she sits, an elderly woman hands her a plate, onto which Jae eagerly adds a bit of everything. "Butter?" asks the woman, passing her a dish and a knife.

"Thank you."

Jae takes her time to enjoy the delicious meal, no longer feeling surprised about anything at all. The people around the table talk in subdued tones amongst themselves, not paying her any special attention. Equally, Jae feels no pressure to introduce herself or start a conversation. Perhaps this is what therapy does to a person: leaves you hungry and fed up with talking.

Swallowing the last of her cherry tomato and spicy lettuce, she sits back in her chair feeling satiated. At last she begins to speak. "So, I've debated with the people of religion, played games with the existentialists, had a nice chat with the Humanists, and laid down for analysis; what can you give me here?"

"Absolutely nothing!" retorts one of the men.

"We don't believe in anything," says another, "certainly nothing supernatural, like a God or an afterlife."

"But isn't no belief in God a belief itself?" asks Jae, genuinely puzzled.

"Is bald a hair colour?" asks the first man, crunching into a raw carrot.

"Is health a disease?" retorts an Asian woman with short, spikey hair.

"Is abstinence a sexual position?" growls a fat man, laughing.

"Bill, she's only just met us!" chides the Asian woman. "What we mean to say," she continues more gently, "is that accusing atheism of being a belief system, or a religion itself, is one of the most common misapprehensions we come across."

A bearded man opposite continues, "the only thing that unites atheists is a **lack** of belief in a God. We do not have a common belief system, a sacred scripture, or an atheist pope. We come from as many different backgrounds and cultures as exist in the world, in as many different shapes and sizes - as you can plainly see from this table."

Jae looks around seeing that indeed everyone in attendance is completely different. Stretching her legs out underneath the table she nibbles a dry crust of bread. "But what about moral values?" she asks.

"Yes, almost everyone asks this question," replies a fair-haired Scandinavian-looking woman. "Religion and ethical behaviour are not even slightly related. Our ethics are based firmly on a sort of enlightened self-interest. We think human beings have the ideas of right and wrong already firmly embedded within them. The desire for co-operation, justice, to give and receive love and acceptance, all come from this innate need. We don't act the right way for fear of mysterious reprisal, or because a horrific punishment may be enacted upon us after we're dead; we do good simply because it's the right thing to do! We value family, society, culture and freedom without being ordered to by some kind of supernatural fantasy image."

It all seems to make sense to Jae, although she finds their replies somewhat rigid, very certain. How can they be so completely sure of themselves? "Don't you have any doubts?"

"No, not really," the fat man continues. "We've contemplated the idea of a god in all its many forms, but decided it just doesn't make an ounce of sense. We think that propounding the idea of a supernatural force of judgement is purely a tool to frighten young children with, and a means of controlling adults. We're simply too logical to believe god is anything more than a fantasy people think they need in order to make themselves behave nicely, or from which to receive comfort in times of sorrow or desperation."

An African man takes up the thread. "We believe that science will one day answer all our questions, even if they can't be answered today. If you look at it historically, you can see that throughout the ages, the role of a god or gods has dramatically decreased in relation to the increase in scientific knowledge. Nowadays god is thought to be a mysterious being beyond the possibility of our knowing, but in the Middle Ages, for example, god was responsible for everything that was not really understood – disease, undesirable weather, acts of nature, and so on."

Jae agrees, "yes, true. But what about that sense of 'otherness'? That feeling that there must be something sacred out there, something timeless, nameless…"

"Well, I understand what you're saying," responds a Chinese man, "but we simply say that it is in our nature as human beings to seek beauty, to thrill at the act of creation, to produce art in all its forms. We don't need a god, or an 'other', to have wonder. God is a non-concept answer to non-questions."

Not completely understanding the answer to the previous query, Jae has one more question for the atheists. "What about the problem of death? If you don't believe in anything after death, how can you live now with the knowledge of such a terrifyingly final end waiting just round the corner?"

"Ah, yes!" replies the blonde woman, "the unbearable yawing gulf of the death of the self. Well, hopefully it's not just around the corner for me!" She smiles and wipes her mouth with a napkin. "Think of it this way: death is complete oblivion. You won't be there to experience it, therefore it does not exist."

Jae sits up in her chair at this astounding thought. *I won't be there when I'm dead, therefore I will never experience death, therefore being dead doesn't exist!*

The woman continues, "if death does not exist, then why should you be afraid of it? Why ruin your life worrying about something you will never experience? As our good friend Epicurus often reminds us, 'death is nothing to us, since while we exist death is not, and when our death occurs, we do not exist.' Our life and death do not overlap. They are mutually exclusive conditions. We will never know it. It's a simple on-off situation."

"But... but that's very interesting!" Jae nods enthusiastically. "You're saying that death is like not being in a room where an event is occurring - which is something that happens every moment of our lives. In other words, why spend time worrying about all the things you're not undergoing or participating in just at this moment? You're not there! You're not experiencing it, so there's nothing to be concerned about."

"You've got it," the blonde woman answers warmly.

Most people around the table have finished eating and are sitting back in their chairs, enjoying the conversation, the mild weather, and the view of the magnificent tree under which they sit.

The Asian man leans forward and speaks earnestly to Jae, "atheism is not a belief in no god, it's just an absence of religion. Our movement seeks the freedom not to support religion through taxes, forced participation, or special privileges. We don't want religion in our lives, but by the same token, we don't seek to convert people to our views. To religious people we say: wear your special clothes, wear your jewellery, celebrate your holidays and pray in your houses, temples or churches. Just don't impose your religion on other people. It's as simple as that."

Holding on to the table and pushing her chair back, balancing on the back two legs, Jae ponders the atheist's words. *"It's as simple as that."* But is it? Nothing of what they've said strikes her as wrong or illogical but she wonders whether, somehow, they too are missing the point. They say they don't have a belief system, but most people with belief systems deny they have them. Surely, the only authentic stance of no belief is, "I don't know." But they don't say this, they are not agnostic. According to them, they already do know. Therefore calling themselves 'atheist' instead of 'agnostic' proves belief is present.

Jae begins excitedly, "in my opinion, you're missing the whole point, because…" but in her enthusiasm, she pushes too hard against the table causing her chair to fall backwards onto the ground. Her shoes forcefully kick the underside of the table as she instinctively tries to stop her fall, giving rise to a sudden loud crashing as cutlery, plates, and dishes rattle against each other.

As Jae lies squirming in the patchy grass the atheists stand up in surprise, and scatter rapidly in different directions across the field. When she finally struggles to her feet she finds herself completely alone, the people, table, and chairs vanished!

Standing stock-still in amazement, her mind and heart race in unison. As she breathes hard and strains to listen, a building sense of expectation forms in the air under the tree. The soft afternoon breeze strokes her skin, and in the stillness a Small Copper butterfly bobs and flits above the grass, searching for a suitable place to alight.

Presently, not knowing what else to do, Jae says out loud, "well that goes to prove it. There's no going back now!"

"Exactly so," an unearthly male voice answers, appearing to come from both inside and outside her body at the same time. "Truth is a pathless land."

Twisting round on the spot, Jae searches for clues to where the speaker could be located. Seeing no-one, she warily responds, "I... think I'm beginning to see that. Shopping for answers in the tent mall of belief is certainly an engrossing pastime, but I don't think it's getting me anywhere."

Scrutinising the field and the distant tents, she continues, "I've slowly come to realise I could be discussing these issues for the rest of my life, endlessly visiting different stalls, discovering the charms and temptations of countless ideologies, but never really progressing beyond deliberation and analysis. Unless of course..."

"Concentrate!" admonishes the voice, interrupting her soliloquy, "cut through the smoke screen erected by thought! Persevere with your fundamental endeavour."

The voice billows out into the air like fog, as if emanating from the very beech tree itself. *Is the tree talking to me?*

"Jae," calls the voice once more, making her jump. "Seek and ye shall find."

Unable to say anything at all, she just stands transfixed, with the quote from her grandmother's note ringing in her ears. A Blue Tit chirrs an alarm call as it flits away from the base of the trunk, disturbed in its hunt for insects. As Jae stands mute, swallowing back a few forlorn tears, the voice continues more sympathetically, "some questions, once asked, cannot be unasked."

"Yes," she croaks, finally finding her voice, "this is my experience."

Then, relaxing a little, she perseveres, "I am seeking. Seeking everywhere I can think of… but," and she sighs, frustrated, "what exactly is the question, and where are the answers?" Glancing around once more, she demands, exasperated, "where are you? **Who** are you?"

Becoming much more matter-of-fact, and now evidently separate from her, the voice replies, "I'm right above you, up here in this wonderful tree!"

Craning her head back, Jae sees a man in a large straw hat sitting in the tree astride a big sturdy bough. "Oh, it's you, it's you!" cries Jae in surprise, recognising the man from her painting.

"Yes, me," he smiles, patting the branch in front of him. "Join me. I'll show you the view."

Jae's face falls, "but there's no way up! The trunk is vast and there are no handholds; I can't climb it."

Crestfallen, she walks round the base of the tree searching for a way to scramble up but sees no possible route, although remains convinced she should try. Moving a little distance away from the tree she shrugs and peers back at the man, perplexed. "I can't…"

"You still need a lot of help," he scolds.

Lowering her gaze to the trunk once more, she suddenly notices a metal ladder leaning up against one side of the tree leading directly up to the branch where the man sits. Running over and starting to climb cautiously, she wonders how she could possibly have missed it. *It wasn't there before, I'm sure of it!*

Reaching the top, she swings her legs over the branch and shuffles nervously forwards on her hands and bottom until she eventually arrives, breathless and relieved, opposite the man in the straw hat. Wrapping her legs around either side of the branch, she clings to it tightly with her thighs and hands, fearful of the drop. They are about three metres above the ground, yet he sits with his back to the trunk, nonchalantly reclining in a devil-may-care pose, arms folded across his chest. In order to see the field with the marquee and tents below her, Jae would now have to twist perilously round, craning almost backwards over her left shoulder, which, she decides, she's definitely not going to do.

"Well I can't see much of anything facing this way," she declares, with a fraudulent laugh that fades almost immediately as she becomes aware of a deep rumbling sound in the distance, not unlike the approach of a stampede of wild beasts. As the noise swells it develops into a thunderous din, making the leaves on the tree around her shake and tremble. Jae clings frantically to the bough, lying down flat on her stomach, gripping the branch with every ounce of her being, her eyes squeezed shut. For a few seconds the frightening pounding seems to comes from directly underneath. A waft of hot, steamy air enfolds her and dust flies up into her nostrils.

And then almost immediately, and to her profound relief, the noise diminishes, gradually dwindling to nothing as the stampede moves away.

"What on earth was that?" she gasps in amazement, sitting up slowly, her eyes darting around in fear. Strangely, the man doesn't seem in the least bit disturbed, still lounging apparently unconcerned against the trunk, smiling casually.

Then, leaning forward and throwing Jae a dramatic, almost gleeful, look he suddenly declares, "behold the view!" and he opens his arms majestically gesturing to the field behind her. Turning her head to the left she realises she can easily see the entire area after all. But all she can make out is a terrible scene of devastation: hoof-prints in the churned up muddy ground, and collapsed, smashed tents. The marquee, tables, and stalls are all flattened and destroyed; pieces of broken wood and flapping, frayed canvas litter the vicinity in dirty chaos.

"What a dreadful mess," she breathes, feeling so grateful she was up in the tree when the stampede occurred.

"On the contrary," replies her companion, "it's an extraordinarily beautiful sight!"

Staring silently at the splintered wood and trampled material left behind by the pounding hooves, Jae lets this statement percolate through layers of her being, not wanting to react instantly. It strikes a chord, resonating with something important within her. *How can the destruction of all that organised information be a lovely thing?*

Then, with a sharp intake of breath she reaches a sudden understanding, and replies, smiling, "why yes; yes I think it is." Shuffling about to find a more comfortable position on the branch, and to avoid a small twig digging into her leg, she continues, "it's a pity, but in the end, however tempting, there's nothing to gain from any kind of external authority is there?"

The man smiles at her.

"I think I've come to realise that there's nothing out there that anyone, or anything, can give me; therefore there's nothing to receive. I'm looking in completely the wrong place," Jae concludes, before finally pronouncing, "if I stay here I'd be a deluded frog at the bottom of a well."

The man in the straw hat leans forward once more, speaking in a low, urgent tone, "so now you've jumped out of the well! You've finally fallen in love with the questions - not the answers. Your horizon is no longer a small circle of sky far above your head, but a large expanse of blue extending in all directions. This is an exciting moment for you. But beware! Nests, distractions, and detours are still everywhere; and not always visible to your puny mind."

Jae nods. "Hmm. Puny? Okay. I can be strong. I **will** be strong. No crutches."

"Congratulations!" announces the man like a town crier. "A successful demolition job has been achieved." But then he becomes more business-like, continuing, "and now our time here is finished."

"What do you mean?"

Pulling an enormous saw from somewhere in his jacket, he turns round to face the trunk and begins to cut vigorously through the branch of the tree on which they're sitting.

"What..? No! What on earth are you doing? Don't chop off our branch - we'll fall! This lovely tree..." Jae wails helplessly, digging her fingernails into the bark and squeezing her legs around the branch as sawdust flies into the air. But it's too late. There's a great creaking and groaning, and she feels herself falling backwards off the branch towards the ground.

Clenching her teeth and bracing for impact, she contracts into the foetal position, surrendering to her fate. As the air fills with tiny particles of fresh green wood, she deeply regrets such vandalism to the great tree.

A few seconds later, she subconsciously registers that there hasn't been an impact when there should have been. The fall seems to have slowed, while at the same time, strangely extended. As she continues plummeting downwards, her eyes closed tightly against the cloud of sawdust, a sudden, unexpected surge of exhilaration flows through her body. She thinks jubilantly: *seek and ye shall find. I'm doing the seeking right now… This is it, granny, I'll never give up!*

The image of the man from her painting blazes in her mind, and as she falls, he smiles and takes off his hat, revealing thick, wavy brown hair. Suddenly the image melts and transforms alarmingly into a steaming, shiny black ox glowering at her in defiance; and in the distance she thinks she hears the sound of a melodic cadence from the Gloria of Beethoven's Mass in C.

CHAPTER THREE

A Resonating Sound

*L*anding unharmed, with a gentle thud, Jae opens her eyes to find she's sitting in a comfortable red velvet seat, in what appears to a medium-sized concert hall. Staring wildly around, she realises she's trapped, hemmed into a row not far from the front by a packed audience occupying every seat in the room. A performance is obviously imminent. The lights are already dimmed, and all around elegantly adorned theatregoers murmur in excited anticipation. By her side, dressed in casual trousers and a light brown sports jacket sits the man from her painting: handsome, groomed and dressed for a concert. With a sharp intake of breath Jae launches into a salvo of questions, but he interrupts almost as soon as she begins, extending his hand towards her.

"Call me Douke," he says in muted tones, his face turned towards the stage.

"Mr. Douke?"

"Don't be silly. Hush, it's beginning."

"But I… How did you… we..?"

"Child's play."

"What?"

"Quiet!" he snaps, causing Jae to frown with exasperation; but she acquiesces and remains silent.

The auditorium lights now fade out completely and an expectant silence descends over the audience. She turns to look at the brightly-lit stage below and watches as a choir and orchestra in formal black attire, rise as one, to their feet. At the same time, a lone man in coattails appears from the wings, walks to centre stage and shakes hands with the lead violinist. Then he turns to face the audience and with a relaxed smile on his face, takes a long, deep bow.

Suddenly Jae feels excited to discover what's going to be performed, and as a gentle, swelling Kyrie begins she instantly recognises Beethoven's Mass in C.

"Oooh, I know this piece very well," she hisses madly in Douke's ear. "We're studying it at choir now!" Douke nods politely, appearing not to be interested in this news preferring instead to concentrate on the music.

Jae subsides into her chair feeling snubbed, and wondering how on earth she's come to be wearing a beautiful blue satin strapless dress with pearl earrings, and a triple-string pearl necklace. However her attention is soon completely captured by the music she knows so intimately. She can't help but sing along under her breath.

Odd, inexplicable, and sometimes frightening things have been happening lately, and it appears there is nothing she can do about it; although at the heart of things she subconsciously recognises she may be dictating events herself. Turning to Douke she means to ask about this point, but is surprised to see he has completely disappeared! Where he was sitting a moment ago there is now only an empty seat.

Scanning quickly round the near vicinity Jae can't see him anywhere, or even anyone who looks like him. *Why would he suddenly get up and leave?!* She feels frustrated and confused. Staring blankly at the orchestra arrayed in a semi-circle around the conductor, she tries to imagine where he might have gone, and why. Realising she's staring exclusively at one of the double-bass players, she re-focuses to see it's none other than Douke himself! Wearing a black tuxedo, white tie and shirt with dark cufflinks, he's sitting on a stool leaning slightly forwards towards the score, an intense expression on his face. She also notices he has closely-cropped dark, almost black, hair.

That's weird. I thought it was longer than that, and brown. And what's he doing down there?!

Jae's attention is captivated by this newly transformed, intense-looking Douke, playing passionately yet not standing out, perfectly blending with his colleagues. *His colleagues? Does he know the other players? Did I only imagine him sitting next to me?*

She sighs and rubs her eyes. It's all very confusing. Sinking her head into her hands she lets the music resonate fully inside her. She wishes she could just rest quietly for a while to clear her mind. But then she thinks: *my mind's been unclear for years. Perhaps here, in this strange place, I'm going to finally get some clarity?*

The performance is enthralling with wonderful top-quality solos and a note-perfect orchestra. As the final "pacem" is gently sung at the end of the Agnus Dei, Jae feels transported into a realm of peace and calm repose. Her previously racing mind has become tranquil and soothed, and a beatific smile softens her expression.

The concert is over, and after a short silence and total stillness on stage, the conductor slowly lowers his baton allowing the audience to break the tension with joyful applause.

Douke stands with the orchestra when signalled to bow, and watching him closely Jae thinks she sees a smile on his face too, although it could be a grimace. He glances up to where she's sitting and winks, causing an unexpected surge of adrenalin to flush through her body.

As the lights brighten over the audience, and everyone around her begins to talk and stand up, Jae realises she doesn't know where to go or what to do next. It must be late afternoon. She wonders whether it would be possible simply to walk back home, cross the bridge over the river and pick up her normal daily life. Could she find her way back to the village in this satin dress, pearl jewellery, and high heels? But that would be giving up, she immediately concludes, remembering her passionate vow on the path earlier to find the answers, to solve this now, today. *I'm not going back until it's over, until I find what I'm looking for. I need to keep going, persevere, continue the journey…*

Standing up decisively, she shuffles along her row and out of the auditorium, making her way through the assembling crowd towards the lobby. She suddenly realises she needs to use the toilet, and following signs for the Ladies she's pleased to discover there's one quite close by. As she approaches, squeezing past couples engrossed in animated conversation, she realises it's a disabled toilet only. However, she's suddenly so desperate that she opens the door and after a guilty glance over her shoulder, slips inside and locks the door. Sitting on the loo, she feels relief to be separated from the crowds and rid of the tight, bursting feeling in her bladder. Gazing distractedly around the cubicle she notices a striking piece of art on the wall; a painting of an elderly white rabbit looking nervous and timid amongst a sea of emerald green grass. It seems a strange choice for a theatre, or for a toilet for that matter. Shrugging she stands up. Restroom cubicle decoration is often inexplicable.

Washing her hands and trying to examine her reflection in an extremely dirty mirror (or is there some kind of bronze tint on the glass?) she begins to sing the Kyrie solo from the Mass. It's a beautiful, quiet start to the piece that continues to build and develop. As she peers without success into the clouded mirror, she can't quite remember how she ended up here in this particular toilet in this particular concert hall, but suspects it could be a necessary step along the path, a bit like visiting the tents in the field. *There is something here I need to discover…*

Shaking the drops from her hands, she notices a scrap of paper with some kind of writing on it stuck to the edge of the sink. Carefully picking it up with her nails she sees it's a label cut out of someone's clothing. It reads 'Sapere Aude,' a design she's never heard of.

"Nothing makes much sense in here," she says out

loud. And none the wiser, drops it into the waste paper basket.

Leaving the toilet and looking uncertainly around, Jae notices the crowds have thinned. Just a few couples linger, shrugging on their coats or waiting for friends to re-join them. Across the room she sees a short man standing alone dressed black coat-tails, and wearing an outlandish top hat and large bow tie. When he catches her eye he abruptly begins to walk purposefully towards her.

"Oh hello, hi," stutters Jae, stepping backwards, taken by surprise as the little man hurriedly approaches. He's walking with such speed and determination that she wonders whether he's actually going to stop at all or just bash right into her. With a little jolt she instantly recognises him as the conductor from the performance she's just attended.

Coming to an abrupt halt only a few inches from her nose, he barks, "we need your help. Our soprano soloist has taken a bad fall coming off stage and we need someone to replace her at this evening's performance. A mutual friend recommends you. Apparently you have a truly beautiful voice. Will you help us?"

"Well, I…" begins Jae, shocked, yet also immediately tempted by the idea. "Actually I do sing; and I do happen to know this piece very well. I've already learnt the solo parts, even the tenor solo actually - although I know I won't be needed for that! I suppose I could do the soprano if you are really desperate…" She realises she's talking far too much, gabbling in fact, and should calm down; but it's strangely difficult because she seems to have become quite mesmerised by the man's large bow tie. It gives the impression of being completely white, and yet she's sure that at the same time she can see large, colourful spots decorating the fabric. *Is it plain white, or is it covered with garish blobs? How can I not be sure which?* Staring at the tie, transfixed, she says softly, "it's very beautiful… the soprano solo…"

Then suddenly, snapping her gaze away, she seems to recover her focus, saying more seriously, "I've never sung solo in a professional capacity before – only as an amateur; I don't know if I'm capable."

"We're assured you are. I wouldn't ask if I wasn't pretty certain. At least come and be heard. We're ready downstairs. I just need to hear you in the hall with the others, and then I'll know for sure."

Smiling and inclining his head, the conductor turns on his heels and strides through the now empty vestibule towards the backstage area. Jae hurries behind him, lifting the hem of her dress, treading carefully in her high heels on the carpet. Soon she's hurrying down a set of marble stairs, then over slippery wood, and finally they reach the laminate surface of the floor backstage. She's panting a little due to the fast pace of the walk, but the conductor appears not to notice. Pushing open a heavy door he stands back, indicating for Jae to walk through onto the stage itself. The lights are on over the audience seats and cleaners are working their way through the rows, picking up pieces of paper, tickets, and other detritus left behind after the matinee performance. On stage, a repetiteur sits at a grand piano placed off to one side. As the conductor walks over to the instrument he smiles back at Jae, indicating for her to stand with them near the piano. Walking gingerly across the stage, Jae imagines it full of people - the lights dimmed over the audience, bright and hot over her…

"Ooh, I'm sorry, I'm not sure I'm ready for this," she stutters in sudden fear, "who told you I could sing…?"

"Nonsense!" scoffs the conductor, "I have it on good authority. Let me hear you now. I will decide whether you're ready or not." Indicating to a small group of people standing around chatting on the other side of the piano, he says, "these are the members of our chamber choir, and of course the three other soloists."

They all smile and greet her pleasantly as she stands stiffly by herself, grinning and nodding apprehensively. The conductor then moves them all into a tight semicircle with a practised gesture of his arms, and someone from the choir hands her an unmarked score.

"We'll start with the Sanctus please, then move on to the Benedictus… and we'll see what else we can squeeze in before we run out of time. Jae, please sing with the chorus to warm up." And with that he turns and signals to the repetiteur to start the small introduction to the beautiful, slow, fourth movement.

"WATCH!" bellows the conductor as they begin to sing the small unaccompanied section at the beginning, nearly making Jae jump out of her skin. This is a place where it's so easy to go flat – a common mistake, and one her choir back at home often makes. However this time it's perfect and the conductor gives them a thumbs-up, "on we go."

As the warm-up movement comes to a close, Jae remembers that the Benedictus requires the soloists to work pretty hard. Standing straight, with her head level and shoulders down, she lightly holds the score high enough so that she can see the conductor, the music and the audience seats, without moving her head.

Singing beautifully, every note clear with unblemished purity, Jae gives an exquisite rendition of the soprano solo that she couldn't previously have dreamed possible. Somehow, she was hardly compelled to glance at the score, knowing and feeling the music without the need for thoughts of technique or worry about what was coming next. The notes came to her naturally, easily, and without obvious effort. She could completely rely on her voice as an instrument, as an artistic tool, which she could play faultlessly. It felt glorious, powerful, accomplished.

Towards the end of the movement, just before the choir launches into the Hosannas, the conductor claps his hands to get everyone to stop, and the choir all stare incredulously at Jae before bursting into spontaneous applause.

Amid cries of, "that was fantastic, amazing," and "brilliant! I've never heard such beautiful singing…" Jae beams in speechless wonder, and then laughs with joy.

"Actually, I didn't know I could sing like that either!" she cries delightedly, slowly recovering from her shock. "It just felt so natural, so real and dare I say, almost easy!" But mutters under her breath, "I can't understand it…"

"Well, I was tipped off," the conductor says brusquely, "and he was obviously right. Listen, I don't think we need to bother with the rest. We have three hours before we have to be back here for tonight's performance." Addressing all the singers he shouts loudly, "that's it, thank you everyone, see you in a couple of hours." And then in an aside to Jae, he whispers confidentially, "you may want to cut your hair." And without waiting for a reply he marches off, mumbling something about the Queen!

"What? My hair?" she exclaims, gathering it up in a bunch and bringing it over her shoulder to stare at it, "but I like it long!"

Turning to the choir she exclaims, "what a really strange guy -" but everyone is dispersing in different directions, collecting water bottles and bags, and dumping scores and spectacles on their seats. Between performances, Jae knows, people tend to make the most of their precious free time. The singers will be rushing off to get something to eat, do a few chores, meet up with family or friends and de-stress before coming back to work.

Suddenly alone in the hall she stands quietly, reflecting on her singing. "I just didn't know I could do it," she mutters incredulously.

"Well I knew," says a playful voice from the shadows; and turning Jae sees Douke walking slowly towards her wearing his dark tuxedo, white shirt and bow tie, clapping and smiling affectionately. "You were tremendous."

"You!" she exclaims.

He stops opposite her and looks intently into her eyes. "Yes. Me."

She concedes, "it **was** good singing, very good. I didn't know I could... I mean, I've never..." But he interrupts before she can launch into a discussion about the sudden, dramatic improvement in her vocal ability.

"Come on; this way. I'm to show you to your

room – there's one reserved backstage just for you."

"Oh," replies Jae, "I'm used to squashing into a backroom with the entire choir and changing in the loos." She giggles, "my own personal room - how nice!" and adds coquettishly, "will you be my servant then?"

"I only serve one person," he replies unexpectedly serious, as they make their way downstairs.

"Oh? Who's that?"

"Have you passed a mirror lately?" he replies bafflingly, as they wind through a corridor passing a row of labelled doors.

"But… you know that's the funny thing," Jae responds, flustered, "I **have** looked in a couple of mirrors recently, but they always seem to be dirty, or dark and obscured."

"Oh," she suddenly remembers, laughing, "I wanted to ask you something… I have so many questions! Firstly, how did…?"

"This is it!" declares Douke abruptly, flinging out his arm and compelling Jae to stop and look at the door beside them. A sign proclaims 'Dressing Room 5 Reserved for Soprano Soloist: Florence Foster Jenkins.' Douke smiles and leans across, turning the handle and flinging open the door. "It's all yours. Do go in…"

Giving Douke a quizzical stare, Jae walks slowly forwards into the carpeted room. Gazing round, she sees a pleasantly furnished suite with a small wardrobe, a sink, and a couch with lots of cushions. On one wall there's a large mirror with lots of lights round it, in front of which sits a long dressing table and a comfortable, padded stool. In the middle of the room is a small round table on which is placed a beautiful bunch of flowers (some kind of gigantic daisies?) a small bowl of fruit, a bottle of wine, and one glass.

"A large, bright mirror!" blurts Jae, "well this is all right…" but a soft click interrupts her before she can finish. Douke has gone. She rushes to the door and yanks it open glaring both ways down the corridor, but there's no sign of him.

"For goodness sake, this is getting annoying!" she protests, retreating back into the dressing room and closing the door.

Standing feeling surprisingly bereft, her gaze rests on the little round table in the centre of the room. Three hours until warm-up. Now could be the perfect time to enjoy some of the fruit, or perhaps a sit down with a glass of wine… *And then to look in the mirror.* Picking up the bottle it feels icy cold. Jae checks the label. It shows a picture of a fearsome black ox rearing up on its hind legs splattering mud into the air, with a prominent bronze-coloured hoop through its nose. Written underneath are the words 'Dancing Bull' in bold black lettering, and just underneath in smaller writing, 'if not now, when?'

"Why, yes," says Jae to herself, breaking the seal as she unscrews the bottle, "definitely now."

She pours herself a glass of crisp white chardonnay, taking it over to the couch to sit back and relax, pondering what might happen later tonight. Her voice has never sounded so good which makes her feel confident and self-possessed. It's a magnificent feeling to know she's truly accomplished, and very satisfying to have others recognise and appreciate her skill. Being admired by her peers is extremely beguiling, leaving her wanting to continue to impress them with repeat performances. After tonight's show, she muses, taking a few more sips, perhaps she and Douke could walk home together. They might fall into a profound conversation about the meaning of life and whether he believes in a religion. As they reach her house he might turn and perhaps he would reach down and...

Gently, serenely, without realising, she slides into a dreamless slumber.

"Lord, what fools these mortals be!"

Jae opens her eyes abruptly, squinting in the artificial light, and blinking rapidly. Bending over her and smiling knowingly, Douke rouses her from sleep.

"Pardon?" she croaks.

"It's a quarter-to-seven, lazy bones. You should warm-up now." Reaching out for her hands, he hauls her up from the couch.

"Warm up? What for?" she asks fuzzily.

Suddenly her hand flies to her mouth, as she remembers, "ooh, yes! The performance. Is it really happening?"

Douke walks over and cracks open the door of her room. Immediately she hears the familiar sounds of voices and instruments tuning, warming up, and practising various tricky sections of music in chaotic cacophony. "In fifteen minutes. Break a leg!"

He smiles, "I must get my fingers going too." And with a slight wave of his hand he leaves her alone.

Too hazy with sleep, she doesn't protest. Making her way over to the bright mirror she peers in at her reflection. Everything's hazy and blurred. After blinking firmly and pressing her eyes with the palms of her hands, the nebulous, foggy effect remains. Doing the best she can under the circumstances, she applies some make-up and adjusts her hair. Although frustrated about not being able to see herself properly, she feels secure and confident about having to sing, amazed that she doesn't feel more nervous or doubtful. *It's a wonderful thing to be confident in your abilities,* she thinks, *to know your voice won't let you down.*

After the rehearsal this afternoon she knows her voice is as good as it can be, and that her knowledge of the music is as thorough as it needs to be. She sings some scales as she re-combs her hair and clips it up tighter, hoping it will look presentable. Her voice is still there. She's still got it. Her main feeling now, is one of excitement and anticipation.

A bell rings in the distance, and a few moments later a woman she hasn't seen before pops her head around the door. "This way please, Florence," she says crisply.

"I'm not Florence!" laughs Jae uncertainly. "I don't think..?"

"Sorry dear," enunciates the woman in a business-like manner. "I'm sure you know best."

"My name is Jae," she says, noticing with admiration that the woman's vivid pink lipstick and nail varnish match perfectly.

Together they hurry out of the dressing room into the corridor. Jae tentatively starts to ask why she was mistaken for someone called Florence, but the woman is walking too far ahead for a proper conversation.

Turning a corner they come to a sudden halt. The way forward is blocked by the other three soloists and the conductor. They stand calmly behind members of the orchestra and a full choir of about eighty men and women. Surprised to see the conductor still wearing his black top-hat, Jae finds herself gesturing to his head, and before she can stop herself she whispers, "are you going to, um..?" But she hesitates to finish the sentence. She's never heard of a musical director in a top hat. Waiting for her to conclude, the conductor stares at her stony-faced, making her strongly regret her question. Feeling embarrassed and taken-aback she tries to rescue the situation. "Er, what I mean is, will you actually be conducting while wearing your...?"

"Don't be silly!" he interrupts sharply, "I always leave it at the door. You, on the other hand, still have long hair."

Jae's eyes open wide and she exclaims, "but why does that matter? It's clipped up. It won't affect my singing. Does it look messy? I couldn't really see in the mirror properly..."

"Shush!" barks the conductor, "it's almost time to go on."

As everyone slowly creeps forward, the last few members of the orchestra disappear through the stage door up ahead. When the soloists approach the door, the woman who came to fetch Jae gently closes it to give time for the orchestra to tune up on stage before the concert begins.

Meanwhile, the conductor reverently lifts his top hat off his unkempt brown hair and positions it lovingly on a specially placed chair just inside the door. As he does so, some money falls on the floor and rolls towards Jae's satin concert shoes. One pound and five pence. Curious, she bends down and picks up the coins, wondering at the odd amount. Then, passing the conductor as she walks into the hall, she drops them into his outstretched hand.

Applause swells for the soloists as they appear on stage. Jae arrives at her place in front of the choir directly behind the orchestra, smiling and self-possessed. She turns her head slightly to the right just in time to see the conductor, still backstage, shoving something into his hatband - presumably the money - before striding confidently out, smiling broadly. As he reaches the podium he turns to face the audience and bows deeply.

Jae glances up to where she was sitting earlier this afternoon, and to her horror sees Douke relaxing and smirking right there, leaning back in his seat.

Adrenalin and panic surge through her body. She suddenly remembers what she's been through to reach this point, how many questions she's asked, the struggles she's had. *What's he doing up there?* She feels terror wash through her body. *What am I doing down here?! Why did I agree to this ridiculous, crazy scheme? He's going to sit there and laugh while I fail spectacularly...*

Jae's legs feel weak, and she wonders whether she's about to faint.

I should have stuck to the path... But it's too late to do anything about her situation now.

Beethoven's Mass in C begins with the choir singing the Kyrie and the soprano solo starting a few bars later. Jae knows there is almost no time to collect her thoughts and calm down before she will be required to sing.

The audience falls silent as the conductor turns his

back to them and raises his hands in a graceful upward sweep, indicating to the choir that they should stand. The performance will start any second! Jae has no option but to prepare herself: affect the correct posture, calm her breathing and relax her shoulders... or it simply won't be possible.

Suddenly, something clarifies in her brain and she blocks out all else but the conductor, emptying her mind and focusing purely on the music. On the conductor's cue, the basses begin their quiet, subdued Kyrie, and within a second or two the rest of choir join the expanding harmony, gradually swelling to *mezzo forte* before receding back down again to *piano*. The orchestra takes over for a few seconds and then comes Jae's entry. Taking a controlled breath, well in time, she suddenly feels a flicker of the same exhilaration, the same ecstatic feeling she had while falling from the tree earlier. *This is it!* she thinks, *I am the music, and the music is me*. Consciousness of everything else disappears as she completely loses herself to the performance.

Entranced, Jae sings through the graceful solos of the Kyrie with magnificent control and restraint; shifting, during the Gloria, to a more melodramatic, yet still delicate execution. Continuing through the exciting solos of the Credo and Benedictus she truly shines, singing with clarity, purity, and great musical intelligence. Then the mood darkens for the first third of the Agnus Dei, until the soloists enter with their Dona Nobis, brightening the character of the music.

She can feel the power of her perfect singing, how it gives her complete control over the music; how the audience love it and how the other musicians and singers are clearly in awe.

She could stay here and be admired, adored, perform again, earn money and have a career. Not only would it give the audience a great deal of pleasure, but it would be doing something she loved. She could be famous for her singing! The temptation is strong, but equally she knows she still needs to learn more from the path she was taking before she came into the concert hall. *I'm not ready yet. This is a distraction…*

And as she nears the end of the piece, she feels a duality creeping back into her heart. *This is not quite working*, thinks Jae. To her horror, her voice sounds a little flat, although no-one else seems to have noticed, and the conductor gives her no sign.

Overall, the performance was sublime, expressive, colourful and appropriately subtle. The applause is long and genuinely appreciative. As she walks off stage for the second time, people cluster around her in the wings, in a hubbub of delighted exclamations. "What artistry! What superb technique! You have such a fine quality of musical understanding…" But the applause accelerates and she's summoned back to the stage once again for a third appearance. A cheer rises up from the audience as she appears, and smiling graciously, she walks steadily back to the centre of the stage. Jae squints up to the place where she thought she saw Douke, but doesn't spot him. The other soloists and conductor have walked in behind her, and they all turn to the audience and bow together. Stooping forward in deep and humble acknowledgement, she suddenly hears a commotion coming from somewhere at the back of the hall. The jarring sound of shouts, crashes and stamping feet is steadily increasing in volume. Freezing in mid-bow, she also clearly hears what seems to be the pounding of galloping hooves and a noisy, rapid snorting. Standing quickly upright in alarm and twisting round, she's just in time to glimpse the hindquarters of a massive ox disappearing off stage to the right, his tail whisking the air behind him! Members of the choir and orchestra have jumped aside and are running away, shouting in confusion. Chairs are knocked over and instruments crash to the floor. General chaos ensues. In the confusion and panic Jae turns back round to face the audience, but all she sees is a vast empty space like a dimly-lit, cavernous, black hall without discernable end.

Instinctively knowing what to do, she walks swiftly and determinedly forward into the darkness, gradually leaving the pandemonium behind. Rapidly passing through the inky shadows of the hall, she emerges outside into bright sunny air. Gone is the flowing ball-gown, the beautiful rope of pearls and her delicate high heels. She's wearing her red t-shirt, beige shorts and comfortable old trainers once more.

Turning back to stare behind her, she sees nothing but open fields. Birds call to each other in the sky above, and a gentle breeze lifts her hair.

Walking away through beautiful daises and dandelions she spies a man lying on his back in the meadow up ahead. He's wearing causal clothing, and a straw hat sits by his side. Wordlessly, she sinks down next to him stretching back placidly in the grass, and closes her eyes with a sigh. Their fingers brush against each other.

Eventually, Jae breaks the amiable silence, "my voice was distorted."

Douke lies undisturbed, his eyes closed. He has a peaceful smile on his face and a blade of grass stuck in his mouth. His untidy brown hair falls away towards the grass, allowing Jae to get a better look at his features as she turns to lie on her side facing him. *Somehow*, she thinks, *he looks like a sculpted male version of me.*

She continues, "I heard the distortion myself, but no-one else seemed to notice. Fame, status, money... that's not what I'm after. I see them only as distractions from the path – although for some people they could last a whole lifetime." Lazily, she strokes her fingers through soft blades grass.

"I admit I did think this was it; that I was finally attaining what I'm looking for, but..." she shakes her head, "it definitely wasn't." Then adds wistfully, "it was fun though."

Douke props himself up on his elbows and pronounces, "true ox in ecstasy of beautiful music. False ox trying to own the music."

"Yes," replies Jae seriously. "I feel like I've had a very narrow escape."

Sitting up fully, Douke holds out his hand to offer her something. "I've brought you a present."

She sits up, taking possession of an apparently empty glass jar! A label on the side reads: 'Summer Breeze.' She opens the lid. There really is nothing inside. Gazing back up at Douke, she shrugs, uncomprehending.

"It's pointless trying to own it," says Douke sympathetically, "there's nothing to own."

Jae places the jar down in the grass beside her. "Yes, I see. But while I was singing, I reached a place where there was no ego, just for a second or two - a brief foray to the edge… It was glorious. However, those truly beautiful moments of being totally taken away, utterly absorbed in the music, disappeared as quickly as they came. I wonder… is there a way to make them last beyond the fleeting..? They were so real at the time. I felt completely alive… I'm beginning to wonder whether this is a way of living that could be established as a natural state in everyday life. A normal life without suffering. Imagine that! I think this might be what I'm after."

"I'm so proud of you," responds Douke, smiling deeply into her eyes. "Seek and ye shall find - you've learnt so much, so quickly." And then after a pause, he continues, "your first glimpse of the true nature of self."

"Just his hindquarters disappearing backstage."

"A glimpse nonetheless."

"I want more."

As if taking his cue from her words, Douke leaps to his feet, holding the glass jar and brushing a few strands of grass from his jacket.

"I'll **have** more," continues Jae in a loud voice, scrambling to her feet, ready for anything.

In a quick and surprisingly powerful movement, Douke suddenly pulls his right arm back behind his head and hurls the jar into the distance.

Peering closely at the point where it lands Jae thinks she sees a small wooden gate. Hastening eagerly towards it, the heat of the sun bearing down on her face and the wonderful smell of wild flowers all around her, she feels a billowing contentment.

She's grateful to have got this far; not to have become trapped within some kind of belief nor seduced by the lures of fame, status, or money.

Douke calls after her, "see you soon." Then more loudly, "and take care."

Take care? she thinks, as she reaches the little wooden gate. *Why?*

But as she places her hand on the latch, she feels a sudden chill as a gust of wind ruffles her hair. Looking up, she spots grey clouds amassing on the horizon.

It's going to rain soon, she thinks, feeling slightly unsettled. And passing through the gate she closes it warily behind her.

CHAPTER FOUR

Submission

*T*he field on the other side of the gate appears much the same as the previous one despite it being a few degrees cooler. Gazing up, she sees the sun is now intermittently obscured behind scudding grey clouds, causing the landscape to shine and then turn overcast in a slow-motion flickering. However, the further she walks, the more she notices rocks and boulders scattered around the landscape. A small, stony path has appeared beneath her feet, which she follows as it meanders through a vale of colourful, fertile meadows.

It looks like the foothills of a mountain range, she thinks apprehensively, hobbling along over the rocks. *I'm not dressed for proper hiking.*

Walking with difficulty, she looks down at her legs and is astonished to see she's now wearing clingy, tight black trousers made of a thin leathery material, high-heeled, peep-toe black ankle boots with laces, and on her top half, a short, restricting leather jacket with the zip fastened up to her neck.

"Whaaaat…?" she exclaims, bending down to feel the trousers on her legs, checking they're real. She feels protected, covered up, as if dressed for combat, but completely confused. "No-wonder I can't walk," she says out loud, admiring her black suede boots, "magnificent, but completely impractical."

Looking up again, absorbing the wonderful panorama of distant rolling mountains and wild grasses, she has the idea that she could be somewhere in Crete. The air is fresh and clean, the views extensive and stunning with scattered grey clouds ink-blotting a bright blue sky.

Squinting a metre or two further along the path, she thinks she sees some horse tack equipment laid out on top of a flat boulder to the right. Closer inspection reveals the implements are more suitable for use with cattle. There is a heavy, kangaroo-hide bullwhip and black leather halter with a long nickel-plated lead chain. Next to them is a small piece of paper with a note that reads, 'Our Tools.'

It makes her think of the sculptor when she first crossed the bridge over the river, "…*with just our simple tools to help us…*" although these are vastly different in nature.

Beyond the boulder, resting on some pebbles on the ground and glinting in the sun, lies what looks like a massive bronze nose-ring, suitable for use on a very large beast.

As understanding dawns, the breath leaves Jae's chest in an abrupt gasp of fear. Her body begins to tremble and her mind fills with panic. Glancing swiftly around, she grabs the utensils and runs to crouch behind a solitary pine tree, tightly gripping the intricately braided handle of the bullwhip. The ten foot lash slowly uncoils, the long, tapered fall and popper trailing dangerously around her feet.

Staring around continuously scanning for danger, she awkwardly stuffs the heavy nose ring into a pocket of her leather jacket and zips it in. Her breath hisses into the quiet air and she anxiously wonders whether the struggle will be long and difficult, whether she'll get hurt and how painful it will be. *I'm going to confront a bull in stilettos and tight leather clothing? I'll be killed! I can't do it... I've never used a whip before, let alone a heavy bronze nose-ring...*

Easing fractionally out from behind the tree she scrutinises the landscape for large animals. Nothing moves, except one or two diving, soaring birds in the immense blue sky. She spies a tiny, thin path leading up through the grass towards a darker hillside, slightly higher in elevation and scattered with pine trees.

Almost faint with fear, but knowing the only way is forward, she steps tentatively out, approaching the path unsteadily on her heels. The sun beats down between cloud breaks and the birds screech and plunge above her. *What kind of birds are they? What kind of place is this? What will I find if I continue seeking..?* Her thoughts swoop and dive, companions to the birds.

Eyes darting to the left and right, she keeps an anxious lookout for a large bull, possibly angry, possibly charging. Her dark leather clothing absorbs the heat, increasing her body temperature causing tiny drops of perspiration to prickle on her forehead and upper lip.

Gaining the narrow stony path she steps forward

carefully in a slightly crouched position, turning her head from side to side, remembering to check behind her. So far so good: there's no sign of a large, wrathful animal. A gentle breeze strokes her face bringing temporary relief.

As a few more minutes pass without crisis or drama, Jae straightens up to ease her aching back and knees, allowing the halter and lead chain to hang loosely from one hand, but with the whip still upraised in the other. There's no sign of a bull or ox anywhere nearby.

Well thank goodness for that, Jae thinks, feeling greatly relieved.

Following the path as it curves round the side of a hill, she suddenly comes across a startling apparition. There, in what appears to be a small volcanic pool, lies Douke wallowing naked and smiling, his dark hair glistening in the sun. The hot water is a slightly opaque milky colour, producing an apparently odourless steam that floats lazily into the air. All around the edge of the pool, spaced out at frequent intervals, scarlet-coloured flags flap fitfully at the top of tall poles. Looking at them fluttering in the wind, which, now she comes to think of it seems to be picking up a little, they look more like ragged red fragments of cloth rather than nice neat flags.

Red rags... thinks Jae distractedly, as her eyes wander back down to the glorious vision of Douke in the pool.

"What are you **doing**?" she splutters stupefied, strands of her hair floating on the hot air like a wild corona around her head.

Smiling, Douke rises gracefully up out of the water standing insouciantly before her, the whole of his glorious body in plain view. Tendrils of steam dissolve against his wet skin, and water drips off the undulating topography of his figure. Unable to look away for even a second, Jae gapes, her breath coming in shallow little puffs. She feels the palms of her hands become moist as she nervously clasps her apparatus of submission. He is the most beautiful male she's ever set eyes on, some kind of replica of an ancient Greek sculpture like The Discus Thrower; an Olympic athlete, a biblical hero, perhaps Michelangelo's David; maybe even a God like Hermes...

She jumps as Douke stoops to flick some water in her direction, interrupting her reverie, "pay attention Ms. Jae."

Stepping slowly forward he calls out in a loud, serious voice, "for a long time I've been living in obscurity in the countryside; but today you have met me. I love it here, the fragrant sweet-smelling grasses, the wild herbs and flowers. Here I am most at home... but you won't let me rest." Looking at her with a rebellious expression he continues, "it will be difficult to drive me out."

Resolutely disregarding the seductive sight of his body Jae feels an uncharacteristic clarity of purpose. "Oh but I will," she says in a low, sensual tone, gently and provocatively swishing the whip over the surface of the shallow water. "I see you now, fully, in all your splendour. I truly **am** amazed by your beauty. But I finally have you in my sights and I'm not going to look away. Not now, not ever." She stares straight at him, challenging.

Continuing his progress through the shallow water towards her, he says in a threatening tone, "my will is stubborn and my wild spirit remains. If you wish to make me pure and obedient you must raise your whip."

Taking a few steps forward Jae carefully enters the warm pool in her constraining apparel, "I know that. And I will. I'll never give up now. I've come too far."

They have approached each other from opposite sides and are now standing within touching distance, able to hear and see the exertion of each other's breath. Clouds of steam float up from the surface of the volcanic pool, enveloping them as they stare unfalteringly into each other's eyes. Transferring the whip to her left hand, together with the bridle and halter, Jae lifts her right hand to lightly touch Douke's wet stomach. His body tenses and hardens in response. Desire is suddenly almost overwhelming. It would be so easy, so pleasurable to succumb, to fall into the water with his arms around her. Setting her jaw she resolutely trails her fingers further down his torso, wrapping her hand carefully but firmly around him. Her gaze does not falter. "I seize you," she whispers intently.

Douke replies in a low voice, but equally unflinching, "I have been in your heart for a long time, wandering freely in its mountains and fields. I can't forget the taste of this world easily."

Jae's eyes close and she stands unmoving, holding him, feeling the pulsing, her lips parted as a feverish lust flushes unrestrained through her. She can sense the heat of him on her face and all the way along her body through her tight, restrictive clothing, down to her feet strapped into her high-heeled shoes immersed in the milky water.

"In that case," Jae replies, smiling, opening her

eyes to look at him once more, "I will throw myself harder, deeper, and even more forcefully into the struggle." She leans forward and lightly kisses his lips. "These are your last moments of freedom. When you're subdued you'll be under my will forever. Forever."

As she speaks she releases him, transferring the whip back into her burning right hand. Staring boldly into his eyes she slowly raises it above her head, but Douke merely continues to stare back completely unmoving, an immodest smirk on his lips. "Now, now," he says goadingly, "don't get uptight."

Incensed, Jae suddenly screams, "don't dare me!" and arcs the whip viciously down behind his back to mercilessly lash his legs, making a loud sonic boom with the thong. But she's too late. In that moment he's gone, and standing on the other side of the pool is a huge, angry black aurochs. This enormous ancient beast, like a gigantic ox or bison, stands two metres tall with massive sweeping horns angled up and forwards. His magnificent head is bent aggressively down, black eyes fixed malevolently on Jae, nostrils flaring as he noisily expels air in a mighty belligerent snort.

Scrabbling away in terror, Jae's high heels wobble dangerously on the pebbles underwater until she reaches the bank and dry land. In her upraised hands she clings to the small and feeble whip and bridle, wondering how she ever thought they might help her subdue the beast. Her legs half bent, arms upraised, with fear flooding her body's internal pathways like molten liquid, she crouches, cowering and whimpering.

Seeing the pugnacious nature of this mighty

creature, gaining crystal-clear sight of his wild essence for the first time, she stands at the summit of fear and emptiness, lingering, wavering. It's terrifying and dangerous; the realisation enormous and shattering. *An elemental beast this spirited, this forceful! How does anyone stand a chance?*

Seeing the enormity of her task in its proper light for the first time, she's intimidated and frightened, but having come this far, can't consider defeat. At this point there are no more choices to be made. To see it, to know it, she feels utterly compelled to restrain and master it.

Across the pool the sweaty flanks of the animal expand and contract with his slow, steady breathing. Snorting into the steamy air he lifts a powerful hoof off the ground a couple of inches, leaving behind in the mud a hoof-print the size of a man's head. Carefully he places it back down again before repeating the ritual with the other foreleg. This is repeated a few times as if marching on the spot to a slow beat, while Jae stands and unconsciously mirrors him on the other side.

Suddenly the aurochs' knees crack as he turns his massive body sideways to begin pacing around the pool towards her, shaking his massive head as he places his hooves easily on familiar ground. Jae stumbles backwards, trembling and gasping, "oh no, oh please, no…," scrambling away from the pool and the terrifying creature, in frantic flinching movements.

Her situation is bleak, but from somewhere deep within her, a tiny flame of defiance silently flickers into life. *I can't ever give up.* This impressive beast has been an honoured guest in her life since she became an adult, but now she wants him to leave for good.

Capitulation would be pointlessly counter-productive, and she'd only have to come back here at a later stage and start again. She knows now that she needs to let the aurochs come to her, and that she will need to leap for her life. But the tiny flame of hope within her heart continues to flicker, giving her courage.

Trying to capitalise on this glimmer of hope she straightens up a few inches, anger and self-pity forming heavy pebbles in her heart, alongside the tiny quivering spark of possibility. But the aurochs sees only a weak and desperate quarry before him, and as he quickens his pace towards her, bellowing a mighty roar of satisfaction, Jae raises her inadequate whip high in the air, the thong hanging straight down behind her back. She lets the bull advance as close as she dare before releasing a wild, despairing scream and simultaneously slicing her hand down forcing the whip to slash through the air towards the aurochs' gigantic back. He is almost upon her, his massive horns pointing directly at her body. Falling backwards in fear, kicking wildly and hopelessly out with her skinny legs, she momentarily loses consciousness. But her eyes snap open again almost immediately as she feels strong hands clasp her back.

Above her, Douke glares into her eyes, his short dark hair slick and groomed, an intense expression on his face. She becomes aware of Latin music swelling around them, a fully orchestrated and triumphal España Cañi.

As Douke lifts her gracefully upright she realises they are about to start dancing together on an empty stage. Lights blaze into her eyes; jubilant, challenging music surrounds her, and in an instant she notices Douke is dressed in shiny black heeled shoes, figure-hugging trousers with an open waistcoat, and a flame red shirt slashed to the waist. Jae's long dark hair is slicked back into a tight ponytail decorated with an extravagant red flower. She wears a clinging black dress with three-quarter length sleeves, decorated in lace with a full black and red skirt cut away to her thighs. Behind, the dress is scooped down to her lower back and she's wearing black and red high-heeled dancing shoes. A red flower is pinned on her chest and she wears large gold hoop earrings in her ears.

She can't see an audience, musicians, nor anyone else. They appear to be completely alone. But the lights are dazzlingly bright, and beyond them she's aware of only an immense void of darkness.

A great charging drum roll announces the start of their dance, and with a commanding air Douke reaches dominantly out to lead her by the hand into the sensational ritual of the Paso Doble. Her breath comes in shallow little gasps as her eyes stare questioningly into his; but he just glowers powerfully back, silent, challenging, defiant, but, she thinks, with a slight edge of insecurity or perhaps even desperation..?

However she doesn't have time to analyse these thoughts, as the thrilling rhythm of virtuoso castanets and coquettish trumpet fills the air with their irresistible summons to dance. Full orchestral backing creates an energetic, almost march-like grandiose melody, propelling them on a journey of passionate interplay; a dramatic performance of challenge and submission told in dance through every inch of their taut bodies.

Douke's hips open and twist away from her,

striking an attitude of continual contrapposto, a reflection of the matador pivoting away from the bull. And yet he maintains fixed on her completely, his attention not wavering for a second, leaving her feeling exposed with nowhere to hide. Blending to his shapes, Jae steps deliberately on the balls of her feet, continuing the story of the dance with her arms and hands; gliding intimately close into his body, then circling away into wild separations, before charging forward once again. They're both very erect making strong lines with their bodies during lifts and drops. Jae's muscular legs circle above her in splits as she's raised over his back and lowered gracefully down to the floor the other side.

As the music dictates, she has dropped to the ground in exaggerated collapse, with Douke standing triumphant over her. But a moment later she's picked up in a very deliberate movement and placed back upright and alone once again. He backs away, indicating with a grand sweep of his arms that she should try again. The fast tempo of the music drives them on and she dances tempestuously, as one possessed, in imitation of a cape flying through the air narrowly avoiding being gored by powerful horns.

Breathing rapidly, sweat prickling on their brows, they approach the end of their dramatic performance. Jae races to keep pace with Douke, her legs and feet shearing down onto the floor, arms swinging out in repeated up-elevations. The carriage of her body arches back yet her hips invariably press forward towards him. Without having slackened her efforts for a moment through all this, the strain is beginning to tell. A little sob escapes her throat.

Suddenly he makes an appel, stamping his shoe on

the stage as if flicking a stone from under his foot, and Jae coils her body around his like a serpent, her hands and fingers trailing a pattern around his torso. And then, in synchrony with the final fanfare, Douke grips her hand and holds it high in elevation, twisting her violently around on the spot until she falls to the ground, clinging to his legs, staring up into his eyes, panting, pleading. As the music ends he bends down and glowers at her menacingly. Neither moves for a few moments, frozen in total silence, gulping for air.

Then he grips her dress at the shoulders thrusting her roughly backwards towards the floor. Grabbing upwards with her hands to try and save herself from falling, she finds nothing to latch on to and with a little cry, collapses, landing in the pool of hot water sinking down beneath the surface. Rising quickly up again, spitting water and gasping, she wipes seaweed-like tangles of hair from her face. She's drenched. Her lacy black and red dress clings to her body like a straitjacket.

Staring wildly around for Douke, rain beats down into her eyes blurring her sight and disturbing the surface of the water. Thunder rolls out from under black, forbidding clouds.

Douke emerges out of the gloom as soaked as she is. He bends down and lifts her partly out of the water, laying her to rest on the bank, half in, half out of the pond. As he advances he unbuttons his trousers and shoves them roughly down his legs. Jae's eyes widen, and she holds her breath as he stands still over her for a moment, flicking water off his hair. Her mind goes blank. There is nothing to say.

He steps out of his trousers altogether allowing them to float discarded and rumpled in the water. Jae watches in slight detachment, raising herself to a half sitting position on the edge of the pool. But Douke kneels in front of her in the water, aggressively shunting her legs apart, while her skirt floats helplessly around her waist on the surface. Her feet remain strapped into her black high-heeled dancing shoes.

Now she wants Douke to continue, to enter her; she wants this desperately, overwhelmingly, but at the same time this knowledge ignites a rage in her heart. Tormented and exhausted she cries a great indignant release into the rain and heaves herself out of the pool. Bending down to pick up the whip she turns and stands over Douke, raising the handle high above her head and, without hesitation, brings it slicing down onto his naked shoulders. In that instant she sees Douke's expression change from one of dominant sexual intent, to blissful repose. As the thong slashes into his skin he slowly closes his eyes, giving the impression of someone completely fulfilled.

Appearing to nod his head fractionally, he turns his face peacefully up towards her whip, which she has raised for a second time.

Disorientated, Jae thinks she hears the gentle whispered words, "yes, re-unite me," echo through her brain, and before the whip lands its target once more, she drops it to the floor in a terrible spasm of doubt and guilt.

Turning away, soaked to the skin, she walks dejectedly into a nearby meadow to think. She finds that she's no longer afraid of Douke, or the ox, but she's admittedly undecided about the best way to handle them. Trudging over the short grassy pasture she notices that the more she walks, the less cold and wet she feels. Her dress isn't as clingy around her legs and her hair doesn't feel as heavy or sodden.

Before long she arrives at an area of grass set up like a shooting range, with a large, long table off to one side festooned with bowls of ripe fruit. Her trainers allow her to walk easily over the uneven tundra, and dressed in her shorts and red t-shirt, she's surprised she doesn't feel at all cold. Glancing up at the sky, she sees the rain has stopped and streaky sunlight is beginning to glimmer through the clouds.

Turning her attention back to the range, she notices that it is composed of four long grassy lanes delineated by low fence partitions. At the far end of each lane, a small wooden signpost has been banged into the ground displaying just a single word: 'habit,' 'conditioning,' 'belief,' and 'ego.'

Puzzled, Jae makes her way to the table realising she's suddenly very hungry. The fruit looks succulent and tender. Choosing a plump-cheeked nectarine she takes large ecstatic bites, relishing its soft flesh, delicate sweet aroma and mouth-watering taste. Juice runs down her chin.

Dropping the stone on the grass, she grabs some green grapes and pops them into her mouth, but almost immediately spits them out again, exclaiming disgustedly, "ugh, sour!"

Suddenly she jerks forward flinching in pain, a burning stinging sensation on the back of her bare legs. Twisting round in outrage she sees Douke holding what looks like a bamboo cane, laughing.

"What are you doing?" she shouts, infuriated.

"I'm just being a good Christian," he answers, shrugging nonchalantly.

Then, all at once, his mood changes and he begins to advance threateningly. Jae backs hastily away along the table, but he bears down on her, the cane upraised in his hand, yelling, "who is going to control whom? What is going to control what? WHO NEEDS THE CANE??"

As she nervously watches his angry face draw closer, time seems to stagnate, and her hearing fail. All becomes silent and inert. She suddenly realises she can take as long as she needs to decide the best way to respond.

Turning unconcernedly away to nibble at some tart little raspberries, she repeats curiously, "who needs the cane?" The raspberries are like super-sour penny sweets - moreish, but at the same time, slightly unpleasant to eat.

"Me? No. Not me – I've rejected distractions, and I won't fall for them again. This is it now! I'm on the path. Surely there's nothing left to reject."

Calmly ignoring Douke, who appears rooted to the spot, frozen in an attitude of wolf-like advance, she joyfully picks up the bullwhip from the table and walks over to the range. Aiming one after the other at the wooden signs, she smashes and splinters the first three with great clashing sonic booms, as the end of the whip exceeds the speed of sound. Coming to the last one, 'ego,' she repeats the process of raising, aiming, and slashing the thong down and out, but at the very last moment Douke is standing in place of the sign and takes the full action of the leather.

As the thong contacts with his skin he transforms instantly into a little black and white puppy, bounding up to Jae, a happy bundle of vivacious energy.

"That is the end of your wild rampaging!" she says

sternly, wagging a finger at him. Now there is no more void! No more loneliness!"

Sliding a collar over his head and clipping the harness firmly in place, the puppy has little option but to sit meekly at her feet. She holds the lead tight.

"Now BEHAVE," she continues unrelentingly, "it's time to go. I have to take you back to your shed."

Swinging round and tugging on the lead, Jae ushers the puppy away, leaving the range behind them as they regain the stony path. Circumnavigating the pool, they head off towards the mountains and dark shadow of the distant pine trees.

CHAPTER FIVE

Ascending to the Pinnacle

Passing through a small wooden gate, Jae - with the puppy energetically pulling in all directions at once – stumbles gradually round the edge of the pine wood; but they make very slow progress. She has constantly to be aware of the puppy darting from left to right, in danger of tripping her up with every step. Luring and praising him all the while, she tries to keep the leash tight but he frequently forges ahead straining to go faster in sudden spurts of energy, then abruptly reverses direction and falls behind causing her to jerk to a stop and twist round.

"For goodness sake, where are your leash manners?" she cries in exasperation, after having had to wait on the spot for a minute to calm him down.

The way ahead leads distinctly upwards and the hills are getting steeper, transforming into proper mountains. A sudden enthusiastic tug sideways could result in a steep tumble down into the valley below. On her left, the side of the hill rises up fairly sharply, too precarious to scramble up with an excitable puppy. The little stony track is their only way forward.

"Sit!" she commands in a firm voice, and the puppy stops abruptly in his tracks, looking up at her. "I'm not going a step further until you behave. You have to stop straining at the lead, yanking me this way and that. I'm in control now, and you do as I say. Understand?"

The puppy rests on his haunches looking glum.

"Good. I'm going to get blisters on my hands if you keep on like this!"

As the puppy sits, obedient and sorry for itself, Jae takes the opportunity to study her surroundings, noticing a kind of plateau not far ahead beyond a clump of trees.

"I think your shed might be up there somewhere," she says more gently. "Let's go and see. Heel!"

And they both start walking again, but this time the puppy seems to understand that he must follow tamely and respectfully.

They trudge uphill together at a steady pace, winding and ascending more rapidly - the path very much the only safe way to proceed. The drop to her right falls more steeply away the further she walks, and it's become completely impossible to ascend the cliff to her left. She holds onto the leash very tightly.

"Good boy," Jae praises the puppy encouragingly, as they safely negotiate an area of loose stones and hostile shrubbery. She's very concerned about keeping the puppy under control, deciding the best way to proceed is for her to walk ahead, leading the way, with him following calmly behind.

"I'm very strict," she says conversationally as they progress along the path. "If you wake up from a nap and whine, I'm going to ignore you. If you jump up at me, I will tell you off. But," and she bends down to stroke him affectionately, "I'm not harsh or cruel. There's a big difference, you know. You're young and full of energy, and I appreciate you don't mean to misbehave. You're only following your nature without thought or censor."

Standing up and tugging the lead to signal they should start walking again, she says, "this is my job, little impressionable puppy. I need to be continually with you, always vigilant, always aware... so I can catch you in the act. A moment later, and it will all be useless!"

Breathing hard, Jae eventually reaches the plateau, a modest area of flatish land composed mainly of very short grass and a few giant boulders. On all sides is a stunning, undulating mountainous panorama, with one or two snowy peaks in silhouette on the far horizon. Over these distant summits the brilliant blue of the sky fades into a white haze, with an almost imperceptible blush of pink. It looks like the point in time when dawn has ended and the day just begun.

Taking a few deep breaths Jae relaxes her shoulders, extends her spine, and fills her lungs with fresh air. She holds the puppy's lead tightly in her right hand, but he gives her no trouble sitting still and obedient, seemingly enjoying the view. Gazing over the wild and rugged landscape she feels a deep contentment swelling out from a central point somewhere in her stomach. This is true splendour.

True magnificence. A place where you can see, and feel, the awesome power and vastness of nature. An empty landscape full to bursting with nothing and everything.

Dropping the dog lead to the ground she stands on it with her right foot and slowly lifts both arms above her head, taking a long slow breath in through her nose. Holding it for a few seconds, she closes her eyes in complete stillness and emptiness, then slowly releases the air through her mouth, simultaneously bringing her arms back down to her sides.

Upon opening her eyes she's surprised to see a little Buddhist monk standing facing her on the plateau. Bowing his shaved head in greeting, he clasps his hands lightly at chest level in a loose fist. Wearing variegated brown-coloured robes, he carries a small wooden begging bowl and has nothing on his feet. After a few seconds he straightens up and smiles at Jae, indicating with his left hand something behind her. Turning round, she sees an old wooden bowl and more brown robes carefully laid out on a flat stone beside a scrubby little bush.

"Welcome to Bliss Point," says the monk, as she turns back to him with a questioning smile, "please put on your robes."

They walk back together towards the flat stone and the monk continues, "these are ancient, traditional robes made of cloth that has been munched by oxen…"

"…munched by oxen?"

"…burned by fire, gnawed by mice, and worn by the dead."

"Worn by the dead?!" squeaks Jae, alarmed.

"Yes," replies the monk in a polite, even tone. "In

some cultures the robes are composed of excrement sweeping cloth; but as it happens, not these."

"Hmm…ah. Oh."

"These useful discarded bits of material have been scavenged from rubbish dumps, roadsides, cremation grounds, and other places. The truly unsalvageable parts have, of course, been trimmed away, but the rest is sewn together and washed, before being dyed with roots, tubers, herbs, bark or flowers and leaves… all sorts of things."

"I see," says Jae hesitantly.

"This is what gives the cloth its brown hue, a sort of earthy, neutral colour – a shade generally considered ugly by society."

All at once Jae understands. "Then I will wear them gladly as a way of symbolising that I reject cultural values."

"They are simple and serviceable and I hope they feel comfortable and fit well," replies the monk. "But as a matter of fact, one doesn't necessarily have to reject…"

"DON'T EVEN THINK ABOUT IT!" shouts Jae to the puppy, who has suddenly started tugging at the lead trying to leap up on the boulder. "I'm watching you all the time now, even if I appear to be fully engrossed in conversation. Sit still! I won't take any nonsense."

The puppy gives up his game and sits down meekly.

The monks smiles, apparently impressed. "Very good," he says, and then turns his back on her to gaze out into the distance.

Taking her cue, Jae slips off her red t-shirt, steps out of her khaki shorts, and puts on the robe. As she does so, the monk chants a simple verse:

"How great the robe of liberation
A formless field of merit.
Wrapping ourselves in Buddha's
Teaching we save all beings."

Jae is pleased to find they fit very well and don't scratch or annoy her; they seem to have been designed perfectly as practical, everyday work clothes. Leaving her trainers, shorts and t-shirt in a neatly folded pile, she picks up the begging bowl, and tugging the lead to make the puppy follow, she joins the monk to stare in wonder over the majestic landscape.

She feels as if she's come home, as if this is where she's always meant to be. *I've found my place at last… this is it!*

Presently the monk interrupts their companionable silence, "come, the people are waiting."

Composed and serene, they walk slowly over to the plateau where Jae, for some reason, is not surprised to see that a considerable crowd of people has gathered. Right now, she feels that anything is possible and nothing would totally amaze her. Off to one side, on top of a small grassy mound, she notices a boulder covered with some kind of thick green vegetation.

"That is where you'll sit," murmurs the monk, "we've made it as comfortable as we can because you might find yourself here for a while."

On top of the boulder the pile of leaves will act as a sort of cushion – Jae sees they are some kind or laurel or bay leaf – and down beside the edge of the stone is a tray with a steaming tea pot and an empty cup.

"I think I'm going to be perfectly catered for," she exclaims joyfully as she settles down cross-legged on the comfortable foliage, pouring herself a cup of green tea. "Piping hot too! Thank you very much."

The little monk bows and smiles saying, "I will leave you now. But remember this: there are none so deaf as those that will not hear, and none so blind as those that will not see." With that he turns and blends into the crowd.

"Oh. Hmmm. None so blind as those..." repeats Jae nodding in appreciation, "yes I understand what I need to do."

Lifting the plain white cup to her lips she sips the refreshing hot tea and loops the puppy's lead around her bare ankle. Looking up she carefully studies her environment. The crowd has inched forward and now, as one, sits cross-legged on the grass in front of her, waiting, anticipating. The sun beats down but isn't too hot, providing the perfect ambient temperature for sitting still without discomfort. She feels as if she understands the whole world, and experiences a profound desire to lead and direct other people, to share her wisdom. But just as she's about to start speaking, a little girl with curly brown hair, wearing jeans and white t-shirt, dashes out of the crowd towards her. As she reaches Jae she bows slightly and hands her three objects: a hand mirror, a string of polished red beads, and a comb in the shape of a dolphin.

In a reverent voice, the little girl says, "I'm Vesta. I've been asked to give you these presents as a thank you for coming here to teach."

Holding up the necklace she continues, "these beads are made from Mediterranean oxblood coral and there are 108 of them on the strand. If you like, you can wear them around your neck or hold them gently in your hand."

"Thank you, Vesta. Oxblood..? They are lovely." Jae takes them carefully, appreciating their rich tone and plump, round shape. "I might wear them now. What beautiful luscious colours..."

Vesta smiles and holds up the hand mirror. "This mirror is for you to see the reflection of your face..."

"About time too!"

"And this is a comb for your hair," Vesta says, handing Jae the dolphin-shaped, wide-toothed comb.

"Well thank you very much, Vesta," Jae responds pleasantly, carefully placing the beads around her own neck. Then, raising the mirror without expectations she gazes, at last, at a clear reflection of her own face. She looks content, at peace, yet full of life. Her brown hair glistens, her dark eyes sparkle, and the earthy wholemeal colour of her robes complement the warm radiance of her features. How strange to see her reflection properly after all this time. She looks so much more relaxed than when she last stared at herself in the living room mirror back at home. And there's no brown tinge or distorted glass on this mirror... but... on closer inspection she does notice a smudge of something on her cheek, like a black smear of mud. Rubbing it gently doesn't remove it, so she dips the end of her sleeve into her cup of tea and tries to wipe it away, but it persists. Whatever it is remains stubbornly in place. Shrugging, she puts the mirror back down on the rock. It can stay there, as can the comb. As can the smudge.

Glancing down to check the puppy remains happily dozing at her feet, she takes a deep breath and begins to address the crowd in a loud, clear voice, "I will help you as much as I can. I can't promise anything sudden or miraculous, but I will do my best to answer your questions, solve your problems, offer advice. I've reached this point after a long and difficult journey, and I will give you one hundred percent of my attention, now in the present, lucid and complete. I am yours for as long as I can give." At this, the people rise to their feet and form an orderly queue, beginning closest to Jae and trailing all around the edge of the plateau and beyond.

Jae takes another long sip of tea as the first person, a blue-eyed, blonde-haired woman wearing a top with a picture of a rabbit on it, steps forward eagerly to ask her question. "Greetings Jae, my name is Freya; I've come all the way from Sweden. My question is: what is love, and how can I achieve a state of permanent loving?"

Without pausing or blinking an eye, Jae responds earnestly, "love is a state of being that is without mind!" And then sits quietly with her eyes closed, hands folded in her lap, the conversation over.

After a short wait, Freya says somewhat incredulously, "that's it? Just no mind?"

Jae nods imperceptibly. "No mind."

"I don't get it."

"If one day you have children, you will understand."

"But I want to understand now, and I may never have children!"

"I think that highly unlikely, Freya," Jae replies deliberately.

"Why? But, wait, are you saying that if I don't have children I will never understand love?"

"What I am saying is that love is beyond the reaches of the mind. It is a state of being that cannot be **achieved**; it just is. It's most easily felt between parent and child, rarely between one adult and another. I cannot describe it to you."

"Oh."

Seeing Freya doesn't understand, Jae continues, "you don't have to worry about whether you love or don't love. When you love, you can't go wrong. Everything you do is perfect."

"Everything I do is…?"

"Perfect. Yes, because love isn't one thing or another. It has no dependents. It can't be sloughed off like a second skin, or changed like clothing. It's an irreversible condition. It **is** your skin. It goes where you go, and can be heard when you speak. Love unavoidably will come out of your mouth. It's not separate from you."

"How do I reach this state?"

"Search me."

"Can you give me any clues..?"

"For starters, don't try to fuse; don't try to attain, or achieve. Just don't try, full-stop. It's not about trying. In love there is no 'me' and 'you.' It's about just being."

"Okay. Thank you, I will think on these things."

"Good luck with your head-banging."

Freya smiles a watery, discontented smile, mumbling, "thank you for your answer," and with a sullen nod of her head she walks past Jae's boulder and disappears off down the hill, petulant and disaffected, resenting the expense and effort she made to get here, only to be confronted by a fake.

A beautiful, older woman in her fifties with curling dark hair and olive skin approaches Jae next. Bowing slightly and looking up at her with intelligent hazel eyes, she says, "my name is Demeter; I'm from Greece, and I would like to know the solution to suffering."

Jae fixes the woman with a benevolent but intense gaze, and after a few seconds replies in a steady voice, "why are you worrying about such things? Wouldn't it be better to just admire the view?"

"I...can't help it," Demeter stammers, "suffering is all around us, it's an everyday experience. There's no getting away from it that I can see, although plenty of people and books tell me there is a life without it. I would like that life."

"Then admire the view!" replies Jae more firmly.

"How can that help me?"

"Let go, breathe deeply; nothing is important."

"But everything is **critically** important to me."

"That's what I said – everything is important."

"But -"

Jae suddenly reaches forward and twists a little twig off the nearby bush holding it up to the woman.

"In the wind of life the twig will get blown about, pushed this way and that way – a strong wind comes along and SNAP!" Jae dramatically snaps the twig in half, "it breaks." Then she reaches down and takes a piece of long grass from the side of the boulder and holds it up. "In the winds of life the grass gets blown about, pushed this way and that way – a strong wind comes along and... (Jae blows ferociously on the blade of grass)... it bends gracefully over, weathering the storm to stand up again afterwards, the same as ever. To avoid suffering you have to be like the grass: bending and flexing with the changing currents of life, adapting and letting go. Don't stand rigid, clinging to ideas, expectations and images, or you will suffer."

"Even if my daughter is abducted?!"

"Even if your daughter is abducted, or murdered, or any other truly dreadful thing that can happen. If you bend with the winds of life then you necessarily minimise suffering. Of course, things can frequently occur that afford you terrible grief, cause you to mourn or be dreadfully angry, and any number of other negative emotions; but if one remembers the analogy of the twig and the grass, and you **are** the blade of grass, suffering is minimised, or doesn't exist. But don't worry too much. It's very unlikely anything awful will happen to your daughter."

"I do worry about her. She is very appealing to men, and headstrong."

"Admire the view over the mountains. If something happens to your daughter, then that is when you should attend to how you feel, and the consequences. Meanwhile, my advice is to observe the magnificent scenery. Nothing else is happening right now. Your daughter is not abducted, but the mountains are breathtakingly beautiful."

A few desolate tears slide down the woman's cheeks. "Thank you. I think I understand."

"May your life go well."

Demeter walks away towards the edge of the plateau without looking back.

Jae takes a sip of tea, still piping hot, and just for a fleeting moment wonders if she's doing the right thing. People don't seem to be finding the answers they want or need from her, but perhaps, on the other hand, this is the kindest thing she can do. Perhaps the truth is not fundamentally what they want, yet it is her job to provide it, no matter what the cost..? She has no time to consider this further, before the next person approaches - an attractive dark-haired young man with a trimmed, curly brown beard. Bowing respectfully, he smiles at Jae and begins, "hello, my name is Tobiah, I'm from Israel -" but then he notices the puppy curled up at the base of the boulder and exclaims, "oooh I love your little dog!"

Eagerly reaching forward, Tobiah ruffles the puppy's fur causing him to leap to his feet and wag his tail enthusiastically, pulling the lead taught. "What a sweet little boy you are," continues Tobiah rubbing the little dog's back, "and such dark black fur!"

At this, Jae glances down and sees that indeed the dog's hair seems to have darkened since she last looked, or perhaps it's a trick of the light? She could have sworn he had some white patches before.

"Calm down. SIT" instructs Jae, pressing down on the puppy's hindquarters, whereupon the puppy immediately subsides quietly onto the grass. Grinning back at Tobiah she says, "he's very obedient - we have a mutual understanding. I issue commands and he carries them out."

"That's great," exclaims Tobiah, "I have an excellent relationship with my hound back at home. But the reason I'm here to see you is because I've heard about your journey and what you've been through, and I plan to undertake something similar. Can you give me some pointers about how to start my own inner pilgrimage? I wish to find truth."

Jae thinks in silence for a moment and then blurts, "if you wish to find truth, ask your dog!"

Surprised, Tobiah responds, "what does he know?"

"A hell of a lot more than you!"

"What do you mean?"

"Well, you're looking for truth, Tobiah. And as long as you continue to do so, you will never locate it, even if you search for ten thousand years! Truth is found in no place, in no creed, no temple, or mosque. You can't travel to find it in some far distant country, or through devotion, in books, or via some great achievement. It is not a thing, and doesn't exist."

Tobiah looks confused. "Truth doesn't exist?"

Jae sighs, and gazes quietly back at him. Suddenly she indicates the wide-toothed comb lying in the short grass at her feet.

"Could you please pass me that dolphin comb?"

He reaches down and picks it up, but is surprised to see it's unusable. Most of the teeth are missing and it looks greasy and dirty.

Tobiah apologises, "I'm sorry, it seems to be broken. There are no teeth and it's really dirty..."

"In that case, pass me the dolphin," Jae replies holding out her hand, deadly serious.

Tobiah looks back down where the comb was and sees nothing but green grass. He gazes back up at Jae, who remains still, hand reaching down towards him expecting... what? An actual dolphin? All he can do is just stand immobilised, dumbfounded, unable to speak or move.

A silence descends onto the plateau, broken only by the occasional cough from a member of the crowd. Eventually Jae relaxes and says, "keep your mind still and your mouth shut; then you might just get somewhere."

Then she continues, "this koan suggests to you to rely on the inconceivable. Let go of **all** pre-conceptions! Take this away and work with it."

Tobiah remains standing unmoving in front of her, a stunned expression on his face.

"Anything else?" she eventually asks.

"No."

"Then may your life go well..." Jae dismisses him; and he walks slowly and somewhat awkwardly beyond her boulder, and descends towards the plateau.

After he's gone, Jae fluffs up the leaves she's sitting on, takes another sip of hot tea, and indicates for the next person to approach. This isn't turning out to be as fulfilling as she thought it might.

An overweight Indian man in his thirties with striking features ambles slowly up and touches his palms together in front of her. He has large ears and a very prominent nose that Jae tries not to look at too closely. He's wearing several brightly-coloured necklaces of differing lengths and impressive cuff bracelets around his wrists. His shirt is open down to several buttons, displaying a fleshy-looking chest.

Jae smiles reassuringly, but before he can start, the man turns aside to cough productively. When he begins speaking it's in a surprisingly deep voice.

"I'm from India. My name is Ganapati. I have heard of your achievements, and my question to you is about wisdom. I wonder, how can I acquire deep wisdom?"

Looking out across the crowd Jae takes a deep breath before asking, "have you had a heart-attack?"

Startled, Ganapti replies, "me? No. Why?"

"So your heart still works fine?"

"To the best of my knowledge."

"Then you are just confused."

Taken aback, Ganapti replies, "I don't feel especially confused, I merely came here to –"

Jae interrupts, "you came here to seek out a guru! To follow a leader, a teacher, to gain something from someone else. Only the person who has lost touch with his vital organs, with his heart, thinks he can find wisdom outside of himself."

"But I –"

"Before breakfast, observe your heart," she interrupts sternly, "everything you need to know is already there. After breakfast, observe your heart. During your morning chores, observe your heart… Listening – silence – is the beginning of wisdom."

After a few moments Ganapati drops to his knees and tries to kiss her feet, but she gently motions him away.

"Dear fellow," she says affectionately, "there is no 'me' or 'you.' There is no 'how.' Wisdom cannot be acquired. You don't need me to tell you anything. Instead, implement complete cessation of thought, and in those moments, listen. Listen to what you already know."

"I'm so grateful," whispers Ganapati, pulling a collection of brightly coloured sweets from his pocket, each wrapped in shiny foil. "These were made by my sisters. Would you like one?"

Jae smiles and takes a sweet, peels off the paper, and pops it into her mouth. "It's delicious. Tastes like watermelon. Thank you."

"You're welcome. And thank you for your answer to my question."

Shuffling about on her leafy boulder Jae watches the man meander away over the edge of the plateau.

Turning back to the crowd she feels restless, as if something's wrong, but can't think what it might be. A creeping feeling of unease washes over her as if something's slipped through a gap in her attention. *These people need me, she thinks justifying her actions, I'm doing a valuable service. They've come from far and wide to hear what I've learnt, and I can't disappoint them. I'm here for them.*

She feels she's found her meaning in life – to teach others, to help enlighten those who meet her, by dialogue, discussion and intellectual exchange. She has had such an amazing experience, such a mind-opening realisation, that she wants to share this with everyone from all corners of the world. Perhaps, she muses, she's not trying hard enough. Maybe she should start up a school when she gets home, to help enable people to live a life at one with the universe…

Just then, a pleasant-looking boy in his early teens with blue eyes and curly blond hair, comes forward, and reverently places Jae's empty tea cup carefully in front of her on the boulder.

"Hello," he says softly, "my name is Lucifer, I've come to pour you a cup of tea."

"Lucifer?!" Jae exclaims with surprise, recoiling a little.

"Yes, as my name implies, I bring you light…"

"But Lucifer is the name of…"

"Not originally. My mother assures me that I am the 'bringer of the dawn light.' I'm the morning star." He smiles sweetly.

Taking the teapot he slowly pours tea into the cup, but when it reaches the rim he keeps pouring and the hot liquid starts to overflow, forming a puddle around the base.

"What are you doing?" cries Jae in astonishment, "you can stop pouring now, thank you, it's reached the top. No more will go in!"

The boy looks up and stares directly into her eyes. "I am showing you your mind," he says mysteriously.

Jae stares at the overflowing tea and the expanding puddle on the boulder slowly widening towards her feet. *A brimming-over cup of tea making a mess… What has this got to do with my mind?*

The boy continues, "the cup represents your mind. You can see it is now completely full. In effect it has closed up. You know so much that there isn't any room for anything more to go in. You think you are a great expert, that you have attained something important. But really your mind has just narrowed. Instead you should aim to be a beginner, to have a beginner's mind. This is just vainglory!"

Jae feels her heart skip a beat, and she abruptly stands up straight on top of her boulder, scattering laurel leaves onto the grass.

"Oh foolish me!" she exclaims, trembling and performing a sincere bow to the boy. "I believe you are right - I see the trap!"

"You have not forgotten your Self," warns the boy, "you've attained nothing. This is just pride, a form of self-worship!"

Dazed and disappointed, Jae remains on top of her boulder, tears flowing from her eyes, nose and mouth.

"Oh, this place is a delusion too," she cries chastened. "It is a mistake to create such lofty ideas around my Self and my supposed achievement. Actually, there is no achievement at all!"

"Where is your puppy?" asks the boy.

Jae looks down and realises she hasn't felt the

presence of the puppy since speaking with Ganapati. He's not there. The lead she went to so much trouble to fit has been severed, and far off in the distance wandering untethered in a field below, Jae spots the shape of a mighty black ox grazing alone and free.

She releases a frustrated little wail and swats her palm against her forehead. Turning to the boy she says remorsefully, "I have been afflicted with self-congratulation at having come so far. Little by little, without noticing, I've come to think greatly of myself and my achievements; but in reality I'm none other than a white elephant. I purport to guide the process, yet I am still stuck myself. How much good can come of this? Confusion upon confusion! How can this help people?"

Taking off her robes and letting them fall in a pile by her feet, she discovers she's wearing her old familiar red t-shirt and khaki shorts underneath. Her trainers are on her feet. Taking the necklace from around her neck and dropping it onto the robes, in a loud voice she speaks to the crowd.

"Better not listen to me – I'm a fraud! I'm merely reading answers off a page. I have nothing of importance to tell you. Goodbye."

Running down the mountainside without a backward glance, she aims roughly in the direction of a little pool of water she spotted, about half way down. As she descends her tears dry on her cheeks.

Delusive concepts just keep coming back. This bad habit must be eliminated!

Arriving at the vicinity of the pool she takes some time to catch her breath, pacing up and down and gathering her thoughts. Then, leaning over the edge carefully holding her hair out of the water, she stares into the crystal-clear water to study her reflection. A persistent breeze disturbs the surface giving her a slightly out of focus appearance. *I didn't mean to boast,* she thinks, frustrated. *I just let my guard down for a moment. Just a few seconds of inattention and this is what happens!*

Seeing the reflection of an ox's head behind her in the water she says out loud, "your nature does not easily change. You have endured over such a long period. Even though I now understand the nature of emptiness, struggle still seems necessary. Or, at least, vigilant and meticulous observation."

Standing up and turning round, she sighs deeply, looking the ox straight in the eyes. "I've had enough of this. I want to go home."

The ox gracefully lowers his head, and placing her trainers near the base of his horns she hops up onto his neck. Clambering lightly and rapidly on all fours she reaches his back, and perches cross-legged, gazing up at the impending sunset.

As the creature turns his massive body away from the pool and begins to walk slowly back to the path, she acknowledges that from now on there will be no need for nose-ring or whip.

CHAPTER SIX

Date Night

With two such intimate friends, spoken directions are not necessary. The ox treads slowly but confidently, following the winding mountain path gradually down, without instruction from Jae. Little stones tremble and scatter under his hooves, and bees fly hastily away as they pass. The trail hugs a moderate slope up the mountain to their right, with a steeper grassy drop down into the valley on their left. Jae begins to see tulips thrusting up amongst the longer grass. There's still the odd large rock either side of the path, but the huge boulders are gone now. Wisps of cloud float in the air above them, made hazy by the yellow dusky light. She feels peaceful.

Soon Jae begins to communicate silently with the ox, exploring her actions, inviting a shared contemplation.

By the time I was up on the mountain I had come to know

why I act as I do, how my thought patterns affect my entire life, but I still did not act any differently! Analytical understanding is not of great value. It's still dealing with events in the past.

The ox replies directly into her mind, without words: *better get used to it.*

I don't want to get used to understanding after the event. What good is that? I could go on my entire life in that way. I might as well become a psychotherapist. It feels to me like a sort of too-late wisdom, an epilogue wisdom that doesn't help prevent repeat mistakes. It takes you up to a certain point, but no further.

Too-late and non-preventative, as may be, replies the ox, *but unless you continue the journey this mediocrity is the last stage. Many people falter here. But don't be unduly concerned; in mediocrity you can be perfectly content, living a happy and apparently fulfilled life. You can leave all this hard work, down tools right now, and go back to your old life where you left off. Use your inheritance to lie on a beach in the Seychelles.*

You can't tempt me! Jae laughs at the ox and his old tricks. *I will never live at the bottom of a well. Having jumped out a few times and seen the possibilities, seen the hugeness of the sky outside that small circle, I will not settle for anything less.*

That's my girl, yawns the ox, apparently unimpressed.

A silence ensues as Jae un-crosses her legs and shifts into a more comfortable position, legs astride the beast's back. She feels the warmth from his body seep into her legs – his skin is almost velvety soft. Above her, violet tones streak the sky as yellow starts to mingle with orange.

The ox is the first to communicate again. *The clearer your experience of having seized me - the more you understand my nature - the harder it is to avoid being bothered and deluded by thoughts that you have attained something. You want to share your knowledge; you want to help people. You become an authority on the subject! Guru Jae. An enviable state indeed.*

I know, you're right. I was proud of what I had achieved. A great enlightenment such as mine needed to be show-cased, shared, acknowledged! I didn't notice this little worm had sneaked inside and made me brazenly boastful and reckless. All along you, headstrong and inexhaustible, were wandering free without constraint. I thought I understood the whole world, but all I was doing was worshipping myself.

They weave their way through a landscape of scattered trees and little scrubby bushes, having gained the lower slopes of the mountains. Not far away she thinks she sees clumps of plum trees bearing fruit, although they don't look fully ripe yet.

Everywhere the grass is tinted a rich rusty colour in the setting sunlight. Gradually, Jae begins to hear the tones of a flute being played somewhere in the distance, a sweet but slightly melancholic tune. It echoes through the hills in a minor key, mellifluous, enthralling and hauntingly beautiful. She closes her eyes to catch every note.

The voice of the ultimate, thinks Jae.

The song of emptiness, agrees the ox. *The sound of what we want.*

Love.

Without the ox proclaiming or saying anything, Jae understands that at the moment, whether walking, sitting, running, laughing or crying, he is always present. No matter where she goes or what she does he is her constant companion. It's always been this way, since she was born.

I don't think I'm ready to part ways with you yet, she thinks, *it's so pleasant, and I'm very happy here. I love you.*

The ox forms only one word: *clinging.*

I don't think it's quite that bad…

Making Jae jump out of her skin, the ox suddenly snorts and bellows, *then show me your original face before your mother and father were born!*

After a perplexed silence holding her breath, she relaxes and rapidly exhales, saying out loud, "you still surprise me."

With a frustrated sigh, she turns round and lies down on the ox's back, her head on his neck, eyes staring directly up to the darkening sky. *Show me your original face…? You mean: what was I like before I became me? But isn't my 'original face' the very thing that I'm looking for? The entire purpose of my journey? My original, true nature… what the hell is that?*

Pfff! If you don't know by now, says the ox dismissively, *you might as well go to sleep.*

And somehow it is perfectly comfortable lying down on the back of the ox. Relaxing without difficulty, finding stillness amid action… Yes, she does need to think for a while, to rest a little now. Closing her eyes, and soothed by the gentle rocking motion as he plods on his way, Jae sinks into a tranquil sleep.

Slowly regaining consciousness, lying with her eyes still closed, Jae notices the rocking motion has changed to become more of a steady vibration, and before she fully wakes, she knows without a shadow of a doubt that she's on a train. Sitting up and swinging her legs onto the floor, she looks around, studying her single-berth sleeping quarters. The blind is up, but through the window she sees only blackness. It's a very small room, with the bed pushed tightly up against one wall and a tiny wash basin under the window. The blind is up over the window, but through the thick glass she sees only blackness.

Suddenly her eye is caught by a pair of elegant black evening shoes placed neatly together under a small towel rail on the opposite wall. Getting up off the bed she slides her feet into the shoes and stares at herself in an oval mirror hanging on the wall. Although the movement of the train makes the glass tremble a little, her reflection is pretty clear. She's wearing an indigo, velvet, mid-length dress with a flattering sweetheart neckline. Her dark brown hair is swept up into a graceful braided bun behind her head, and a delicate silver necklace lightly encircles her throat. Astonished, but pleased with her looks, she picks up a sparkly blue clutch-bag from the end of the bed, opens the door and leaves the room.

Outside all is quiet. She's standing in the middle of a long, narrow corridor. Looking to her right and left offers no clue as to which is the best way to go. In both directions everything is interchangeable. On one side, large windows look out onto darkness, and on the other, neutral cream walls lead to the end of the carriage where a cream door opens into the next, presumably identical, carriage. Carefully closing the door of her berth she notes the room number: six.

Shrugging, she heads off down the corridor in one direction, the black windows on her left, doors to other cabins on her right. She thinks: *I wonder if there are there any other passengers?*

Reaching the end of the narrow corridor she pushes open the adjoining door, passing through a small lobby area with toilets and exits, then on through another carriage door. With great delight she finds she's stepped into the dining car, where a few other passengers sit talking quietly, looking at menus, or eating their meals. Jae heads optimistically towards an empty two-seater table and sits down, placing her clutch-bag near the window. Glancing through the menu, she quickly decides on a mushroom pasta dish with a Greek side salad, plus a nice glass of dry white wine. After the waiter takes her order she relaxes back in her seat feeling ecstatic. *I'm on my way home. The wine's on order. I'm about to eat!*

Closing her eyes she takes a deep breath, leaning her head against the headrest. *It's not always necessary to verbalise what is within, she thinks. Silence can definitely be golden. I would like to see Chloe again. I want to hold her in my arms and smell her. I think my search is ending…*

Opening her eyes slowly, she gazes contentedly out of the window at the blurry blackness. She has no idea where she is, but indisputably she's travelling across great distance at speed. She notes the peculiar contrast between the civilised, every-day business going on inside the carriage – people ordering a meal, bright lights, muted conversation… and the sensation of towns, countryside, whole lives, all flying past at breakneck speed outside. It's nothing but noise, violence and energy out there, while inside it's tranquil and calm. Here, the clink of a knife on a plate, the quiet buzz of people chatting, and the vibration of muffled footsteps as somebody passes.

A man catches her eye and smiles at her in the reflection. Snapping round and staring across the table, she sees Douke sitting opposite her, dressed in a white shirt and indigo jacket to match the colour of her dress. He looks handsome… with a ready smile and slicked back dark hair.

"You're **still** here?!" Jae exclaims, confused.

"I'm still here. I will follow you everywhere, day by day, hour by hour," replies Douke in a serious voice. "We are together. Harmonious."

Jae stares at him, speechless, as the waiter arrives with her wine. Acting normal and calm, Douke requests another glass for himself and the same food as Jae.

Recovering from her surprise and re-organising her thoughts, she says, "actually I'm glad. I didn't think we'd see each other again."

"It's okay, the struggle is finally over. We're in complete accord with one another."

Nodding, she replies, "I think so too. It's untroubled between us now."

They sit in silence for a while as Jae sips her wine and the waiter reappears with a glass for Douke.

"Cheers," he says, and winks at her.

Ignoring the leap in her heart as she responds to his flirtation, she declares, "I **do** feel free, but I think I want you to stay. I'm on my way home. Will you come with me?"

He leans towards her and gently takes her hand in his. "I will stay with you forever."

The touch of his hand is electrifying. She clasps his hand tightly, feeling the constraining, immovable barrier of the table between them.

"I want to merge with you," she says in a low voice full of passion, "I want there to be no hindrances at all."

"All in good time," he murmurs seductively.

Presently, the waiter returns with plates of steaming hot pasta, which he carefully arranges in front of them, forcing Jae and Douke to let go of each other's hands. "I'm sorry for the slight delay," he says apologetically, "I hope you enjoy your meal."

"Thank you," they both reply. And with the tension broken, they unfold their napkins onto their laps and begin to eat.

The food is delicious. Taking their time, savouring every moment, they discuss recent events in detail.

Douke begins, almost accusingly, "you made a fateful decision on a walk beside the river, not long after the death of your grandmother."

"Yes, I did," replies Jae. "By then I had to know **beyond doubt**, whether I, myself, was alive or dead! I couldn't carry on the way I was, not being sure of anything, plagued by questions, without any answers… going nowhere. I needed to clarify the intent of my life, the point of living."

"This challenge came from you, from deep within you. It was something you decided had to be done. No-one issued you orders or compelled you to act the way you did. It was your choice."

"I know that!" Jae replies, wondering what he's getting at. It feels almost as if he's blaming her for something.

"This is, of course, the **only** way in which it's possible to start the journey, your pilgrimage. The search for the footprints can't even begin until the questions arise. Before that point you're merely living in the gloom on automatic pilot. The questions are the lights slowly starting to flicker on."

Then he continues in a more menacing tone, "but freedom comes with a price."

Jae maintains her light and positive attitude. "I know. No crutches. No religion, no beliefs. No fame or wealth - or at least no attachment to them. No hankering, yearning, and striving any more…"

"And not just that," Douke interjects, "it's a sure-fire way of losing friends and feeling isolated."

"I don't feel especially…" Jae begins, but stops almost immediately, suddenly unsure.

"Yes, painful though it is," Douke continues, "and attached though one becomes to the process, even the search itself must come to an end. Walking the Way, becoming an ox herder, is akin to renouncing everything, and then after that, renouncing renunciation."

"Mmm," Jae eventually nods in agreement. "Now that I've asked all the questions and found all the answers, I realise they're all of absolutely no consequence anyway."

Douke raises one eyebrow, "you've found all the answers…?"

Jae stops eating and puts down her knife and fork to take up her wine glass. She thinks about this for a few moments while savouring her drink.

"You're right. Not **all** the answers – if there are any, even." She smiles knowingly. "Before, I felt empty, confused, hopelessly bewildered about which way to turn. I thought I might find the answers to my problems in religion. I wanted spirituality in my life."

She takes another sip before continuing, "although there was much beauty to commend them, I have concluded the religions were each offering a similar thing. And the same goes for the other beliefs and other actions or behaviours. To cede wisdom to an external authority isn't the way to free the mind, it is a way only to further enclose it."

"Clever girl!" cries Douke, "external authority of

any kind, however it manifests, is always limiting." He wipes his mouth with his napkin, "it's one of the very first steps to overcome."

"And then came the music," breathes Jae, wistfully, "oh, it was glorious to be the owner of such a fabulous voice! But as wonderful as it was, I realised that's not actually what I was after either. Had I stayed, sooner or later, I would have had to start at the beginning again."

"Yes, at that point you were ready to **seize** your true nature." He looks at Jae meaningfully for a few seconds, a glint in his eye, before turning away and muttering to her reflection in the window, "that was my favourite stage."

"I hear you!" she teases. "But now you're not just a veneer of pleasant manners and suave good looks, with wildness raging dangerously inside! The calmness I have instilled goes bone-deep."

"I'm truly glad," he replies, seriously, turning back to her across the table.

"What an extraordinary struggle you put up though," she says, lingering a while longer on the events at the mountain pool.

Douke says nothing, regarding her steadily. He knows that at each moment there are all possibilities. Jae can choose any path at any time. He waits, ready...

"But next," Jae continues firmly, as if awakening from a mini-trance, side-stepping dangerous nostalgia, "the fatal cocktail of idealism and wisdom. Such an easy trap to fall into, so beguiling. It must be a really common mistake, don't you think?"

"Hmmm, yes," agrees Douke, taking his cue from her changing disposition, mirroring her from moment to moment, "it's easily done. At this stage you can't help but congratulate yourself on your great achievement. You want to share your apparent enlightenment with the world. In your eager self-worship you want to help everyone, save all souls!"

Jae looks sheepish. "Probably, people get stuck at this stage for the rest of their lives…"

"No doubt. It's pretty tragic," Douke affirms. "Obviously, a wisdom verified only by itself is no good to anyone."

"Yes, another external authority, except this time I **was** that authority." She scrapes her plate finishing off the last of her pasta. "There are traps everywhere, are there not? Probably even here on this train." She glances around as if expecting to see something menacing in the dining car. "Maintaining intensity of attention is dreadfully hard work."

"Until it becomes second nature," says Douke.

"Until it becomes nature."

"Quite so."

And then impulsively, she asks, "is it my nature?"

Looking across at her with fire in his eyes, Douke bangs his knife and fork down onto his plate and scornfully demands, "are you asking me a question?"

Abashed, Jae retorts, "no… not really. I know what I am. I don't need you to tell me. I just wondered whether… you…" she trails off into an embarrassed stutter.

Suddenly he leans forward and explains in a compassionate voice, "my dearest, darling girl, what you are doing is not by any means unique. These questions have been reflected upon for millennia, and will continue to be explored for as long as humanity exists. The quest for meaning, the desire for

137

spirituality, and finally the renunciation of search itself… all this is part of the human condition. If you're lucky, you'll become a person of the way at some point in your life. It depends on how purposefully you push through the thickets, how much energy you give to the hunt, how passionately you want the truth."

A little indignantly Jae begins, "I merely wanted to know if you thought…"

"You cannot search for what matters," he exclaims in an exasperated voice, "leave it aside, you can't own the birds!"

Jae stands up abruptly, banging her hip roughly on the side of the table. She winces with discomfort, both physical and psychological. *Why is he being so rude?*

"Put away your mirror, empty your mind!" he scoffs, almost taunting, as she turns to rush along the corridor to the Ladies.

But he continues, calling after her, "why still seeking purpose? Why still so many words..?"

Jae dives into the toilet and locks the door behind her. She needs to get away from him, straighten out her thoughts. Avoiding the mirror she sits down on the loo with her head in her hands and thinks. *If I abandon search I will never see him again. When will I truly understand that there are still traps everywhere! I still cling for dear life to the root sticking out of the side of the cliff, my whole body dangling over the edge with a sheer drop below. At each stage I always think this is it; but this is never it! I need to let go of the root…*

Once again, to be sure of her approaching decision, Jae replays her experiences, slowly, logically.

In the beginning, after her grandmother died, she was lost. Everywhere she looked she saw confusion and uncertainty. Eventually, questions filled her eyes to such an extent that she couldn't see her way forward any more. She soon came to feel that there was no longer any possibility of carrying on as she was – the desire to dispel her more-or-less continual state of discontented melancholia had become overwhelming. So one spring day, born out of this growing, inescapable need to resolve her doubts, she began her search.

During her time wandering the way she found no answers at all, which, after a while, began to reassure her. Truth, she had come to understand, is not a thing that you can go off and find somewhere. There is no set path to it because it doesn't exist as a thing. Rather, it just comes to you, as a state of being, when you're ready.

Feeling reassured, she stands up to wash her hands and continues her silent line of enquiry. Truth isn't a treasure to be uncovered somewhere like a pot of gold at the end of a rainbow. It doesn't reside anywhere in particular, not in religion, dogma, behaviour, belief. Truth is a state of being which seems to arise precisely when the mind – that oppressive, raucous birthplace of religion, dogma, behavior and belief – is **absent**.

Jae sighs. The mind is an ever-present limiting agency of division, composed merely of forces of judgement, habit, memory, and ego, and yet it is placed on such a high pedestal in our society. However, Jae has seen for herself, admittedly only briefly, that without all this noise a silence can be discovered that is a true vanishing of self. An authentic and piercing perception of what is. This is the truth! And it is to be found – no, not found – **realised**, in no other place than her own no-self!

Hastily plucking sheets of paper from the dispenser she excitedly ponders the idea of the absence of mind. Truth – this place without the workings of mind, allows you to just see, just listen, just eat, laugh, get drunk, work, play and so on. It goes far beyond the emptiness others have indicated they might have found briefly in prayer, or in moments of silent communion with nature. Undoubtedly those moments are true, but as quickly as they come, they're gone again. A flame lit for only a few seconds before being blown out. Too brief and transitory... *Lasting truth is what I'm after...*

Rushing back out of the toilet, she returns to their table and Douke, who is still sitting alone in his seat, waiting. The empty plates and glasses have been removed and her bag sits where she left it next to the window. As she advances, he looks up at her quizzically, almost sadly, as if he knows a decision has been made. Without saying, or thinking anything, she bends down, with her eyes closed, and gently kisses him on the lips. The kiss lasts for several seconds, time stretching out into a void, as they two become one.

Then she stands next to him, her hand on his shoulder. Looking up at her with tears in his eyes, Douke says "we're travelling, on the way, returning, but we're not getting anywhere. What's stopping us from actually arriving? What's keeping you from being home?"

"It's because there is still a 'me' and a 'you.' There is still a self and an ox, separate albeit in complete harmony."

They stare at each other in silence, which she eventually breaks with, "looking for the ox, spotting the footprints, glimpsing the hindquarters, seeing him fully, seizing him, controlling and subduing him… and then…"

"Yes," Douke replies sorrowfully, "aloneness is the natural state for an ox-herder. Accepting this is tricky."

"And then," Jae continues, resolute, "transcending the ox. Realising that he does not exist."

At that moment, the noise and momentum of the train changes suddenly as the brakes are applied. She grabs the handle at the back of Douke's seat to prevent herself from falling forward as the train rapidly reduces speed.

"So no more clinging then?" asks Douke twisting round to look into her eyes.

Jae smiles regretfully. "No more clinging. How can I cleave to something that does not exist? This has to be goodbye."

Douke states in a quiet, level voice, "I die."

Jae says nothing as she leans over, opens her bag and takes out her mobile phone. Then, without looking back at Douke, she turns away and walks towards the end of the carriage.

"At least let me carry you down onto the platform," Douke pleads a little, following her up the aisle, "let me carry you, one more time. Like I always have."

As Jae reaches the doors, the train enters the last stage of its deceleration, before coming to a complete halt in the field by the river. She reaches out and turns the handle, opening the door into the night air.

"I'm leaving now. I am alone. I fully accept this. It's the only possible way to continue; to stop travelling and actually arrive."

Suddenly Douke leans out and thrusts the whip and halter into her hands. "These are the instruments of control you used to contain me. Perhaps keep them in the corner of your room as a memory."

"I don't need them any more," she says, smiling fondly, tucking them under her arm. "But I'll take them as a token."

And taking a deep breath, she descends the steps and strides out across the grass with her comfortable trainers. The night air is refreshing but not cold even dressed in only shorts and a t-shirt.

"It's mild out," she says to no-one in particular, and continues on her way.

CHAPTER SEVEN

At Home

Walking peacefully along the river back to the house, inhaling the balmy evening air, Jae's mind is still. She enjoys the silence and the high-contrast black and grey appearance of everything. The strange muffled noises of the night. A small full moon shines silver and very bright, high above her in the dark sky. Not a single wisp of cloud obscures her field of vision. *This exquisite, clear view was attainable all the time,* she thinks, *the moon just needed to emerge from behind the bank of clouds to reveal what was always here...*

Arriving home she inserts her key into the lock, opens the front door and steps into the muted, sleeping house.

Making her way upstairs, she quietly opens Chloe's bedroom door and slips inside. Approaching the bed, she sees her daughter's inert form spread-eagled across the duvet. One leg and arm stick out, and her mouth is open displaying her slightly buck teeth. The defencelessness of the pose immediately touches Jae's heart and she feels a rush of tenderness for her child. Kneeling gently on the floor by her bed, she kisses the little girl tenderly on the cheek, and whispers, "I love you," before pulling the cover over her limbs tucking her in. Chloe shifts in her sleep and turns over, away from her mother, resettling. Jae smoothes down the child's hair feeling the attractive round curve of the back of her head, still babyish, vulnerable. Then, kissing her one last time she takes her leave, closing the door soundlessly behind her.

Back in her own bedroom, Jae takes off her clothes, puts on her pyjamas and climbs into bed feeling utterly content. *To be is to be related,* she thinks, and drifts off to sleep.

Waking the next morning, Jae hurries to open the curtains and look out at the magnolia. As suspected, the buds have started to crack, writhing froth-like within themselves. All over the tree, creamy pink petals can be glimpsed, although still wrapped closed and capsule-like.

Any day now… thinks Jae joyfully.

Putting on her slippers and picking up her iPad from the bedside table, she potters downstairs to get the kettle going. Sipping tea and eating toast and honey, she skims through all the latest posts in her newsfeed. Clicking on her status box, on impulse she writes, 'hello world.'

Closing her iPad, and leaving her cup and plate in the sink, she returns upstairs to Chloe's room. Her parents, who have both taken early retirement, don't generally emerge until they've left the house. Jae thinks they do this deliberately to avoid the morning noise and rush – not that it's unbearably raucous, but there's almost always something remembered at the last minute, then an ensuing panic and rush-around to find it. As they get older, her parents have definitely begun to prefer a more predictable, calm pace of life, although unexpectedly having a young child back in the household has temporarily scuppered this wish. Jae sometimes wonders whether it was really fair to move back in with them, despite their offer, bringing all her clutter and noise into their sedate and settled lives. As she opens Chloe's bedroom door, she thinks she should give some thought as to how much longer she should stay here, imposing on the kindness of her parents.

Bending down and gently shaking her daughter's shoulders, she says, "time to wake up now darling." Chloe makes strained, groaning sounds as if in deep distress, but this doesn't put mum off. "Yes, I know you're tired and it's a bit fresh this morning, but once you're up, dressed, and have eaten breakfast you'll feel fine. The sun is shining! It's a lovely day.

"Come on, get up please," she says more firmly, and leaves the room.

A little later, taking Chloe to school, mother and daughter walk together, holding hands in agreeable silence. Jae still feels a sense of deep contentment and she's pretty sure Chloe recognises, perhaps unconsciously, that something important has changed within her mother, although she makes no reference to it.

Walking back home along the river she enjoys nature's excitement. Spring means everything is full of potential – buds, birds, insects, colours. Even the air smells of possibility and new beginnings. Somehow, the mechanism of spring seems to have transferred itself into her own soul.

I'm having my own personal spring, she thinks. *I feel about ready to burst.*

There and then, she becomes aware that for the first time in months, there are no questions nagging at her consciousness. It's a truly wonderful deliverance! Her all-consuming need to search for answers appears to be over. *I am free...*

Arriving back at home, she cheerfully greets her parents who sit together at the kitchen table, enjoying a quiet breakfast. Newspapers, plates, a breadboard and tea cups litter the sides. Getting a fresh cup and pouring herself some tea, she feels as if she's ever so slightly intruding on something private and self-contained.

"Did you have a nice time last night?" her mother asks agreeably.

"Hmmm," Jae replies wondering how she can possibly explain her recent experiences. "It wasn't exactly **nice**..."

"Oh dear, I'm sorry to hear that. It was supposed to be your treat night away – a night of complete relaxation. Didn't it work? Didn't you make the most of it?" her mother appears quite concerned.

"I... Oh, yes I did, very much so... but..." Jae feels confused about what to say. She vaguely remembers that yesterday Justin had arranged to have Chloe after school, and her parents had promised to do the bedtime routine in order to let her, Jae, have a rare afternoon and evening completely free.

"Is there something wrong?" her parents look at her anxiously.

Over the last few months, they've watched their daughter become more and more distant and introverted, especially since Vivian's death. Feeling somewhat helpless, they've been more troubled than they'd like to admit about Jae's increasingly fragile state of mind.

"No, no," laughs Jae reassuringly, "nothing's wrong at all. I feel **great.** And I totally loved my time out. I can't tell you how much I appreciate it! It's just that I really can't describe it as merely 'nice.' It was more like mind-blowing." She gives them a genuine smile of joy.

Comforted and pleasantly surprised, her parents exchange a meaningful look, nodding at each other before resuming their breakfast. Their daughter has been acting stressed and unhappy for months, so it's good to see her more relaxed. Her mother thinks: *she needs more time off like this to be alone. Perhaps we can do this for her once a month...?*

"More bread anyone?" asks Jae, picking up the breadknife.

Later, after her father has settled in the living room with the newspaper and her mother decamped for the shops, Jae decides the best thing to do with her time is to sort through her belongings.

Going through everything in her room, all the cupboards and shelves, and then the wardrobe in Chloe's room, she makes three large, satisfying piles of unwanted, un-needed items to either take to charity, offer to friends or, if they're completely unusable, throw away. She finds superfluous knick-knacks, ornaments she no longer likes, collections of magazines she doesn't read, clothes that no longer fit and broken or redundant toys.

"Nothing lacking, nothing extra," she says out loud, admiring the orderly heaps and feeling a great sense of achievement.

Looking again at the charity pile she wonders with incredulity how she acquired so many mirrors over the years. At least three can be disposed of. There's a grey and white cut-glass octagonal mirror on her bedroom wall that she's rather fond of and wants to keep, but the others are definitely surplus to requirements. The mounds of unwanted stuff even include a couple of small coffee tables. She's amazed at how many possessions she's been hauling around all this time. *How did I accumulate so many things?!* she thinks, exasperated. When her mum returns home she vows to load them all into the car and take them to charity that very afternoon.

Walking into the hall on her way to the bathroom, she passes the painting of the pastoral scene she only properly looked at the other morning, but now she's sure the man in the picture is actually the man from her dream – the dark-haired, intense man, the double bass player from the concert.

Standing facing away from the viewer next to the bull, with his hand peacefully draped over its back, the man is turning his head slightly towards Jae, as if to glance backwards over his shoulder from where he's come. His dark hair is cropped closely to his head and the whip hangs loose and unused in his left hand. He looks wistful and handsome.

"Oh Douke!" cries Jae in a tender voice, reaching up to gently touch the painting, "you, the bull – you're still on the path."

While Jae has at last abandoned the journey and her search for meaning, Douke, she thinks, will always be going somewhere seeking something, never at rest.

The sky in the painting no longer appears forbidding and moody; it seems brighter, lighter, creating a more up-beat tone overall. No storms lurk on the horizon. Poppies and wild daisies blaze in the grass, reflecting the brilliance of the sun.

Carefully taking the painting down, she places it in the bottom of the wardrobe in her bedroom, canvas facing the wall. She's not ready to walk casually past it on a daily basis, although she now adores it. *I'll hang it in a proper place some other time*, she thinks.

As she walks downstairs the doorbell rings. Hastening to answer first so her father doesn't have to get up from his chair, she's surprised to see Justin standing there, hands in pockets, blinking in the sun.

"Hi, Justin!" she smiles, brightly. "I thought it was the postman. Why aren't you at work?"

"I took the day off," he says stiffly, a dispassionate look in his eyes.

Jae instantly gets the feeling something's wrong. She leans forward and gives him a kiss on the cheek, but almost imperceptibly he draws away at the last minute, her lips only just making contact with his skin.

"Come in," she says, concerned, holding open the door and following him into the kitchen. She switches the kettle on and gets cups from the draining board, dropping a peppermint tea bag into each one.

Justin sits down at the kitchen table watching her.

He has mousey blonde hair which he wears quite long and swept back from his face, and recently he's allowed a stubbly beard to grow on his chin. He looks at her intensely giving her a tight smile. In that moment Jae loves him deeply. They've been partners for six years and have created Chloe together, so she feels they've grown to know each other quite well. She recognises something important is bothering him now.

"What's up, Justin?"

"Jae," he starts, a little hesitantly, "I know you're going through something right now. I don't know what it is, but you're pretty distant and withdrawn…"

"I'm really sor…" Jae begins

"Hold on," Justin interrupts. "Something's taking place inside your head that's pretty radical, and although I'm right here trying to understand you, you don't ask me for help or try and talk to me about anything… Do you have a problem with us?"

Pouring boiling water into each cup and bringing them over to the table, Jae smiles deeply, sitting down next to him. "I can explain everything. It's okay now. It's actually all over. Don't worry. I'm aware I was completely preoccupied for a while, I'll admit that. I had so many questions… Oh Justin, I've got so much to tell you!" she squeezes his arm affectionately. "But within myself, I need you to know, I've finished with all that now."

"Really?" Justin replies, amazed. "Just like that?"

"Yes, really. Just like that. I'm back. I've been somewhere – I don't know where, I can't really describe it… but I'm back now."

She places her hand over his in a tender gesture of reassurance and sincerity. Responding, he turns his hand over, lightly holding her fingers.

"I see," he says looking confused. "I…I'm sorry but I'm not quite finished with what I was saying. I wasn't expecting you to say that! I'm really glad to hear you feel recovered from whatever it was you were going through, but… it has had an impact on me, on us; and all this time I've been trying to sort it out in my head. What I need right now is a bit of space."

"Space..?" Jae repeats anxiously, "space for what?"

He lets go of her hand and sighs, leaning back in his chair. "I just need some time alone to think a few things over."

"Think what over? I told you, I'm back. You can talk to me now. I mean, I will listen and talk to you… I want to tell you everything!" she speaks quite fast, eagerly.

But Justin continues in a firm voice, "I appreciate that, I really do; and if you'd only said that a few weeks ago, maybe I'd be willing, I'd be able to engage… but right now, as I said, I really need a bit of space."

"To think about… our relationship?"

"Yes."

"Oh."

They sip their tea in silence for a while, Jae's mind a blank. This announcement has come as a complete surprise. She hadn't imagined he would feel like this. But in truth she hadn't really thought much about Justin at all. Or anyone. In fact, she privately admits that she's been very self-absorbed lately, preoccupied with her internal questions and troubles, unable to perceive the impact her behaviour might have had on others.

Eventually she says in a steady voice, "I understand; and I agree. I have been distant - I fully acknowledge that. I think I withdrew from our relationship, maybe even from life itself for a while. Even Chloe noticed something strange was going on with me. After Granny died I just had so many questions. Her death really shook me. I sometimes felt like I, myself, wasn't properly alive. I was full of doubts and felt restless and uneasy, engrossed in a kind of internal conversation or argument... do you understand what I'm trying to say?"

Justin reaches out for her hand again. "I know it hit you hard; I'm really sorry for your loss. I know how it hurts. But... you didn't share any of this at the time; you completely failed to communicate with me on every level other than the superficial. You didn't come to me for comfort, to talk, or for anything. You just became more and more distant and focused on what was going on inside you. It was like you put up walls around your emotional inner self that I couldn't scale."

"I know. I'm sorry. You're right, but... I've changed! That's all finished. I really feel completely different now. I've worked some things through and the way I currently feel is completely opposite to the way I felt a few weeks ago. And the change is permanent. I feel it in my heart."

"I...I'm glad for you," Justin replies trying to stay strong, determined not to be swayed from his decision, "but... I still think I need a break. While you were absent, I thought about it a lot and now I've decided. I don't want it to be over between us, I'm not saying I don't want to be with you, quite the opposite. I would love us to be a family again soon, just us three - although not like this with you living here at your parents' house."

He drains his tea and pushing his chair back he suddenly stands up. "In the meantime I need some space just to be by myself." And with that he slowly turns and walks out of the kitchen.

"Okay. I totally understand," Jae says humbly, "come back and talk to me - when you're ready."

"I will. I'm sorry. Goodbye for now."

At the front door they hug briefly, and Jae clasps him to her, inhaling the familiar smell of his laundry detergent. "I'm sorry. Please think seriously about the fact that I've gone through some kind of fundamental transformation. Not wanting to get too deep about it, I do feel as if I've had a kind of deliverance - that I've been saved from a life of mediocrity! I want to share this with you, but you haven't given me a chance, since it happened, to talk about it."

Unable to keep the excitement from her voice she continues, "Justin, it feels like a liberation, like a light has switched permanently on in my brain. It's a big deal! I want to tell you..."

"You do seem different," he concedes, stepping outside and firmly bringing the conversation to an end. "I think you've revealed more to me this morning than you've shared in the last few months."

"Oh gosh, I am sorry," Jae can only repeat her genuinely apology, "I didn't mean to withdraw. I didn't even realise I was acting like that. I couldn't see myself from the outside. Why didn't you ask me about it?"

"I did, Jae, but you weren't listening," he replies, turning aside.

And with a brief wave he walks away from the

house towards the pavement, the fully-laden magnolia tree still and unnoticed off to the side. Jae closes the front door and stands still for a few moments, then rapidly opens the front door again. She can see Justin disappearing round the bend, and opens her mouth to shout something to bring him back and engage him once more; but then she stops, changing her mind immediately. She doesn't want to fall into the trap of forcibly trying to choreograph events, attempting to control his, or her, life.

Leave him, she thinks. *He needs space. Give him what he asks for.*

Releasing her breath and closing the front door quietly, she walks slowly upstairs and sits on her bed.

Space simply means space. It doesn't mean the end of the relationship, that it's over for ever, or in fact anything other than simply 'space.' It merely means he wants some time alone. Things are exactly as they are - no more, no less.

She picks up her phone, sticks some earphones in her ears, and fires up her MP3 player allowing it to randomly choose something. It's the 'Et in Terra Pax' movement of Vivaldi's 'Gloria' recorded by Trevor Pinnock in the 1970s. One of her favourites – a mournful, almost grieving, haunting score oddly set by Vivaldi to pleasant, uplifting and positive words. The entire movement comprises just one repeated phrase: 'et in terra pax hominibus bonae voluntatis,' which Jae remembers means something like, 'and on earth peace to people of good will.' Perfectly cheerful words, yet the finished product sounds deeply sorrowful and plaintive. Was Vivaldi indicating that elation can be found amid anguish, and by the same token, anguish within moments of elation? Jae knows that this is absolutely true.

She lies slowly back on her bed, closing her eyes and letting the music wash into her soul. *The best thing I can do now,* she thinks, *the only thing I should do, is give Justin the space he asks for.*

If she tries to pressure him, change his mind, ask him to explain himself, it will only encourage him to pull further away. She can't alter his thinking nor change his ideas. He wants time away from her to sort out his thoughts, to come to a decision about their relationship on his own. The worst thing she could do would be to try to influence or dominate him, attempting to force him to see things through her eyes, from her point of view. As she's recently learnt so vividly, the best route to true understanding is through a personal discovery of one's own, in one's own time.

I really have changed, she thinks serenely. *I've been through something profound. I've had some kind of a realisation, an alteration of my fundamental way of being and thinking. I feel it and know it deep down in my soul. Chains have been broken, restraints released, blinkers ripped off! Justin needs to go on his own journey and experience it for himself. It's nothing to do with me.*

Jae believes Justin has genuinely sensed her transformation, but that he is confused. She wonders whether, after the break, he'll want to get to know the 'new' Jae - the Jae that was always there, that she went to such great lengths to seek, find, subdue, harness, and eventually release. *The Me that I thought I had lost, but was there all along, and that, on closer inspection, doesn't exist at all!*

For Jae, it's a brand new intelligence. A completely different way of being, not just of seeing, or of understanding, but a penetrating awareness of the mechanics of mind, self and thought in the present moment.

Loving Justin properly is to respect what he needs and to allow him this request. No clinging.

Taking out her earphones as the Vivaldi comes to an end, she gazes through the window at the magnolia just about to burst into blossom. The tree is there, as ever, quietly getting on with its life, doing what it needs to do - not trying to influence anyone, alter the world or change things to suit itself. It just does what it does, growing slowly, sinking its roots deeply and gently into the earth below, taking in nutrition, moisture, light, and transforming them into energy which it uses to enlarge and blossom, without restraint, into the air. And then, of their own free will, and simply because it's right, the birds come happily to sit on its branches and sing. No-one forces, pressurises or begs the birds to come – they just do because the environment is right. For them, it's the best possible place to be.

In the spirit of the magnolia tree, Jae releases all anxiety and fear from her mind, enabling her to continue to just be herself, get on with her life, go to choir, look after Chloe… and wait to see whether Justin comes back.

She thinks: *if I possess him, I do not love him. If I think I own him and can control him, I do not love him. If I love him I set him free. He will come back and sing on my branches if he wants to. I don't have to persuade him. I don't have to fight to alter his way of thinking. I don't have to cling or attach. This is real love, and it is as unrestricted, strong and final as death.*

Smiling and feeling a great sense of wonder and gladness spread throughout her soul, she thinks, *this is wisdom*. This is true intelligence... living without the intrusion of thought, without the clamorous chattering of the mind.

She walks towards the small mantelpiece over the little chimney to the right of the window, and lights a scented candle with a match. *I must be a light to myself, always,* she pledges, *this is my work from now on.*

Lifting her head joyfully to gaze into the clear, reflective octagonal mirror on the wall, she catches her breath in a wave of devastating ecstasy that expands out from her stomach to enfold and embrace the world. There is no longer opinion, view, belief, duality; no separation between observer and observed... The ox does not exist, has never existed. Jae herself ceases to exist as a separate entity from the sky, the tree, the house, humanity. Awareness swells out from her like an atomic explosion, to encompass the distant reaches of the universe, body limitations ending... This is to know true love and compassion for all humanity. The ending of self, the dissolution of all barriers, an eternal, absolutely incorruptible observation leading to genuine understanding without judgement, without motive.

Loving all humanity.

Save all souls...

Enraptured and trembling, she gently collapses back down on her bed, slowly becoming still, feeling the entire world as her body...

CHAPTER EIGHT

No Thing

By what authority?

CHAPTER NINE

Returning to the Source

*L*ying motionless on her bed, Jae opens her eyes feeling a diminishing sense of loss, as if she were struggling to view a momentous and glorious image through a gauze veil; but even as she pushes the gauze aside to stare at it without obstruction, the image vanishes, leaving her with only the memory of a concept. After a few seconds of struggle she releases it to the ether: the moment has passed. Trying to contain and define an ineffable experience is a fruitless endeavour, and immediately Jae realises this is also true for every moment of her life.

I have been somewhere, she thinks peacefully, allowing consciousness to seep back into her being, *I can't say where, I can't describe or communicate it… but **there** I have been…*

Sitting up on the bed she stretches and gets up. The piles of organised unwanted items on the floor look wonderful to her eyes. Early afternoon sunlight flooding in through the window strikes the carpet - a simple and completely unremarkable, ordinary occurrence, yet it fills her heart with a boundless joy. The little flame she lit on the mantelpiece appears homely and welcoming. Never before have things seemed to her so perfect; just as they should be.

Leaving the room she walks downstairs into the kitchen, with each step feeling more and more grounded in reality, back in business, home for good. Making a cup of green tea and some marmalade toast, she sits at the kitchen table silently eating, the warm food and drink bringing her fully back into the present moment. After she's finished, she puts on her shoes and coat and hurries outside to collect Chloe from school.

Waiting at the school gates, mingling with the other parents, Jae chats briefly to one or two mums she knows, and then Chloe arrives in a gush of noise and energy. Bounding up to Jae and talking rapidly while rummaging in her book bag, she accidentally drops her coat on the ground. Jae squats down to pick up the coat and gets lured into admiring each of the drawings and paintings Chloe produces, one after the other from her bag, with great pride and a big smile on her face. After this they have a quick hug, before putting the artwork back in the bag and heading off home. During the walk, Jae's role is mostly to listen while Chloe chatters continuously about her day without seeming to take a breath. Presently they stop beside the river to gather stones and throw them into the water.

"Here's a big one," says Jae passing Chloe a large stone. It makes a satisfying 'plop' as it drops into the water. Chloe cheers, "that was the best one ever!"

As they move away they almost stumble into the fresh remains of a dead rabbit.

"Aarrrggghh!" shouts Chloe, backing away and refusing to walk on.

"Don't be afraid," Jae says gently, "it's dead, it can't hurt you."

Chloe shakes her head and squeezes her eyes tight shut.

"Look, it's not really scary. You can see a little bit inside its body - the pink, brown and red are just organs and a bit of blood. It's just a dead creature, nothing more."

"I don't like it," moans Chloe, refusing to budge.

"But this is part of life," explains Jae, "things live and things die. It's what happens to all things. Everything comes to an end. Nothing is permanent my darling. It's a cycle: starting out, like you are, with your whole life ahead of you, then blossoming, like me…" she winks at her daughter, "and then growing and maturing like granny and grandpa… and eventually ageing, and finally dying and decaying. It's natural."

"I'm frightened of it."

"That's okay, Chloe. Shall I hold your hand so you can go round it?"

"Thank you, mummy."

They skirt carefully round the dead rabbit together and continue on their way.

"Try not to think about death too much. All it means is 'an end.' Everything in the entire world has an end. But for you it's so far ahead in the distance, such a long, long time in the future, that you can't even imagine how far! Instead of thinking and talking about it, let's forget about it and decide what we want to do when we get home. Which games or toys shall we play with? Dominoes? Dolls? Carrot and Donkey?"

Her attention diverted, Chloe begins to rattle off suggestions for games. But just before they reach the house, Chloe looks up at Jae and says, "mummy…?"

Jae knows that she is required to ask, "yes?" in an interested tone of voice.

Chloe quietly states, "you don't think too much any more, do you?"

Bending down to hug her closely, Jae swallows back a sudden surge of emotion, replying, "no. No I don't. I've stopped doing that now, thank goodness. I want to play with you more instead. Life is precious and fun, and we don't want to use up too much time in boring old thinking!"

At home they take off their shoes and go into the kitchen. Chloe sits at the table as usual, getting the things out of her book bag again with a steady commentary, while Jae prepares a snack and a drink.

Later, at bed time, Jae asks Chloe whether, for a change, she might be allowed choose a story this evening. Delightedly Chloe accepts, and Jae goes to get the book she's been thinking about since they saw the dead rabbit on the walk home from school.

"This is a book called 'The Wind in the Willows,' and I want to read you a short bit from chapter seven, which is called 'The Piper at the Gates of Dawn.' It's about two friends - who are a rat and a mole - going on a journey together. Mole is rowing them in a boat on the river so they can search for an otter that's gone missing. All of a sudden something strange happens to them. Afterwards, they're trying to remember exactly what it was that happened. It might be a little bit difficult to understand, but just listen to it while I read, and you can tell me what you think of it afterwards. Okay? Try and concentrate on the words, and what sort of image or feeling they give you. Lie back and relax, darling…"

As Chloe settles back against her pillow cuddling her fluffy pink unicorn, Jae sits on the edge of the bed and begins to read:

> 'I feel strangely tired, Rat,' said the Mole, leaning wearily over his oars as the boat drifted. 'It's being up all night, you'll say, perhaps; but that's nothing. We do as much half the nights of the week at this time of the year. No; I feel as if I had been through something very exciting and rather terrible, and it was just over; and yet nothing particular has happened.'
>
> 'Or something very surprising and splendid and beautiful,' murmured the Rat, leaning back and closing his eyes. 'I feel just as you do, Mole; simply dead tired, though not body tired. It's lucky we've got the stream with us, to take us home. Isn't it jolly to feel the sun again, soaking into one's bones! And hark to the wind playing in the reeds!'
>
> 'It's like music… far away music,' said the Mole nodding drowsily.
>
> 'So I was thinking,' murmured the

Rat, dreamful and languid. 'Dance-music... the lilting sort that runs on without a stop... but with words in it, too... it passes into words and out of them again... I catch them at intervals... then it is dance-music once more, and then nothing but the reeds' soft thin whispering.'

'You hear better than I,' said the Mole sadly. 'I cannot catch the words.'

'Let me try and give you them,' said the Rat softly, his eyes still closed. 'Now it is turning into words again... faint but clear...

'Lest the awe should dwell
And turn your frolic to fret,
You shall look on my power
At the helping hour,
But then you shall forget!'

Now the reeds take it up... forget, forget, they sigh, and it dies away in a rustle and a whisper. Then the voice returns...

'Lest limbs be reddened and rent
I spring the trap that is set.
As I loose the snare
you may glimpse me there,
For surely you shall forget!'

'Row nearer, Mole, nearer to the reeds! It is hard to catch and grows each minute fainter.'

'Helper and healer, I cheer
Small waifs in the woodland wet,
Strays I find in it,
wounds I bind in it
Bidding them all forget!'

'Nearer, Mole, nearer! No, it is no good; the song has died away into reed-talk.'

'But what do the words mean?' asked the wondering Mole.

'That I do not know,' said the Rat simply. 'I passed them on to you as they reached me. Ah! now they return again, and this time full and clear! This time, at last, it is the real, the unmistakable thing, simple... passionate... perfect...'

'Well, let's have it, then,' said the Mole, after he had waited patiently for a few minutes, half-dozing in the hot sun.

But no answer came. He looked, and understood the silence. With a smile of much happiness on his face, and something of a listening look still lingering there, the weary Rat was fast asleep.

After a short silence Jae asks gently, "what do you think?"

"It's nice. Funny. They are forgetting something…"

"It's a happy feeling isn't it? Two friends quietly chatting and drifting downstream in their boat. Take that idea, Chloe, of a beautiful far-away music that lulls you to sleep, and makes you forget anything scary."

"Ok mumma," yawns Chloe; and Jae kisses her on her forehead, tucks her up in bed, and leaves the room with the door open.

Downstairs Jae finds her parents reading the newspapers in companionable silence. It won't be long now before her mother stands up, goes into the kitchen to make a coffee, and disappears upstairs to watch her programmes. It happens almost every night at around 8:00pm.

Sitting down in a corner of the settee with her legs curled underneath her, Jae says, "we saw a dead rabbit on the path by the river today."

"Ugh!" says her father.

"Oh dear," says her mother, "what happened?"

"Chloe didn't like it. I think it frightened her. We talked about the concept of death again, briefly. As you know, we spoke about it quite a lot after granny died, but this was a pretty graphic illustration."

"Yuk."

"Yes, but the strange thing is, a week or so ago, I wouldn't have discussed these things with her; it would have been too difficult and awkward, especially with granny having died. But now I feel totally able to; and also, that it's the right thing to do. We came across something real and horrible, and it presented an opportunity to briefly discuss the topic once more."

"It's good you kept it brief," says her mother.

"Yes, definitely. Although it raised some interesting thoughts for me. However, with Chloe, I didn't want to start off down a great, long philosophical track about how we can live with death every day of our lives, as an absolute fact, and have it be a blessing rather than something to fear…"

Her father rolls his eyes and rattles his newspaper as Jae begins what he thinks of as an unnecessarily complex conversation, and her mother interjects, "Oh Jae, definitely not appropriate for a six year old."

"I don't know…" Jae seems unconvinced, "well anyway, we moved on and it was fine. We also read something different this evening for the bedtime story, something of my choice."

Jae's mother stands up. "I think I might go and make a coffee," she says, as if it's something that everyone might be interested in, and that doesn't happen every evening at this time. To Jae's continual disappointment, her parents are never interested in any kind of philosophical discussion, usually changing the subject or removing themselves from the room whenever Jae introduces more metaphysical or theoretical themes to the conversation.

"I think I'll go for a walk in the garden then," Jae decides, and takes a cardigan from the coat pegs in the hall. Stepping into her beige trainers, she quietly closes the front door behind her and thrusts her hands into her pockets. She wonders why her parents are never interested in participating in serious discourse or dialogue with her. Do they find it threatening? Boring? A waste of time? Is it personal to just her and privately they have fantastic long philosophical conversations with their friends? Perhaps they're worried that any kind of free-ranging, undefined debate could easily slide into a vitriolic family argument, leaving everyone feeling angry and upset. *But that's not what I want at all,* she thinks; and sighs. She knows she needs to accept her parents for who they are and not force the issue. Justin always likes to debate, and she has plenty of discussion with him. She corrects herself, **had** plenty of discussion with him… *when will he want to talk again?* she wonders.

It's not exactly cold tonight, but it doesn't feel quite as warm as it was the previous evening. Spring is like that, Jae thinks. *At any moment a cold spell can roll back over the Atlantic making everyone shiver in their optimistic thin cotton t-shirts.* Although she's wearing jeans and a long-sleeved top, she's grateful she thought to put on her cardigan.

Heading for the magnolia tree, she takes a deep breath of fresh night air and marvels at the beauty of the evening world. Living in a village they have the great benefit of not being affected by noise or light pollution at night. Consequentially, evenings can be wonderfully quiet and dark, although it's never pitch black right next to the house because of the streetlight on the corner, which softly illuminates the front path and garden.

As she passes under the spreading canopy of the sleeping magnolia tree, Jae is astonished to hear someone singing what sounds like a beseeching love song. At first, she can only catch the general theme of the tune, but as she stops to listen it becomes louder, clearer, and she can start to distinguish the words. It appears to be coming from very close by, perhaps a neighbour's garden or an open upstairs window? Entranced, Jae steps eagerly out again from underneath the tree, only to find that an eerie mist seems to have risen from the grass, obscuring her view.

Disorientated, she stands motionless yet full of life, her ears sending out invisible radar to fuse with the music. The strange, impenetrable fog engulfs the whole of the front garden and beyond, and now she can plainly hear the words of the refrain as a solitary tenor continues to serenade in the opaque evening air:

> "Softly, pleading, flows my singing
> Through the night to you.
> Down to that still copse entreating,
> Love, I'll wait for you.
> Slender whispering treetops rustle
> in the moonlit glade.
> Of a traitor's hostile listening,
> don't, my love, be afraid."

Overpoweringly drawn towards the music, Jae fumbles her way round the side of the house, mesmerised, enthralled, feeling an urgent desire to catch every word as the song continues. Groping her way carefully through the gloom, her arms and hands outstretched in front of her, she navigates the narrow part of the garden close to the next-door neighbour's fence. Somehow this area of land seems much wider than she remembers it. However, at present, she's quite unable to concentrate on perplexing details such as the changed width of the side garden - the potent allure of the song compels her irresistibly on:

"Do you hear the nightingales singing?
Ah, they implore thee.
With their notes and sweet complaining
now they plead for me.
Well they know the heart's desire
well know love's pains,
Touching with their silver lyre
all heart's finest strains."

Proceeding incredulously past an unfamiliar cluster of fruit trees, Jae marvels at how many there are. She's pretty sure they only have two fruiting apple trees, and possibly one plum, if it's still alive, but this is more like an orchard. Did she somehow pass into the neighbour's garden without realising? But how could she have walked through the fence? Bewildered, she advances a few more paces wondering where she's going to end up.

The strange mist continues to obscure her sight and she realises with some anxiety that she has no idea how to get back to the front door. The singing is fading now – Jae can no longer identify the words – and finally it dwindles to nothing, leaving only an expectant silence in its wake.

Wondering what to do next, and in the absence of a better idea, she continues slowly walking forward, peering around in wonder at this new ethereal garden. The mist is beginning to dissolve, and is being superseded by a subtle golden glow which suffuses the garden with a kind of hazy late-afternoon sunshine. *Sunshine in the middle of the night? What is this place..?*

As the last tendrils of mist slowly melt away, luscious colours start to emerge, sharp and crisp in this bright new land. Astounded, Jae spots exquisite flowers of all kinds, hybrid musk roses, white angel's-tears narcissus, magenta orchids, and clumps of flowering herbs - dazzling purple oregano, and delicate mauve puffballs of chives. She stares in all directions, turning round and round on the spot, incredulous and elated.

All at once, she becomes aware of an intense, intoxicating fragrance of some kind of flowering shrub, or perhaps several. A sweet, pink, honey scent, velvety and soft, billows around her intensifying, ascending, leading her with each successive breath toward a mini-crest of aromatic joy. As she turns her head from side to side, inhaling rapidly, she gets the impression of being not quite able to capture the complete essence; of needing just one more sniff of air to fully grasp the aroma. The instant she can say to herself, "yes, this is it," it vanishes, and she has to inhale again. But now, underneath the initial lighter tone, she can sense a darker, richer more musky smell, like cedarwood or distant orange. Oh such elation, such blissful pungent euphoria! Just at this moment Jae can't imagine any reason to ever move from the spot and forsake the rapture of this aromatic apotheosis.

However, soon the gentle sound of trickling water catches her attention, and taking a few last breaths of the sweet-smelling air, she persuades herself to leave, walking away through a little meadow of lush green grass. Just a short distance ahead she comes upon a crystal-clear freshwater spring percolating directly up from the ground. It forms a wonderful, transparent feeder pool to four rivulets that run off in different directions, bordered on either side by yellow flag iris and diaphanous lobelia cardinalis. No more than six inches deep and just a few metres across, the translucent surface of the pool is dotted here and there with brightly-coloured flowers. Jae stares in joyful amazement at beautiful 'pink sensation' water lilies basking on the surface, their rhombus petals sprinkled with countless sparkling droplets that subtly reflect the light in every direction. Her humble garden has somehow become a mysterious and enchanting paradise, a captivating world of breathtaking flora and fauna.

"It's the source!" she cries out, spellbound and somewhat lost for words, "the origin!"

Over on the far side she can see lush pastures strewn with beautiful flowers leading off into the distance. Bright orange dahlias and pink tulips emerge from the ground, ornamenting the grass. Nearby, a particularly exotic-looking flower which Jae has never seen before catches her attention; and she bends down to examine it more closely. It has shards or spikes of orange and blue petals sticking straight up into the air like hair, and underneath an arrow-like green capsule from which it has obviously recently emerged. Standing up and gazing round at the numinous landscape, she thinks, *this is the most beautiful garden in the world!*

Exploring beyond the pool she passes under glossy, full-flowering pomegranate trees, coming upon a charming little brick-built hut. An ancient purple wisteria adorns its sides with delicate, tinsel-like blossoms arching down on slender stems, voluptuously overlapping each other. But the aqueous whispering of one of the four little streams draws her back again to the water's edge. Following its meandering course, Jae hears the calls of numerous birds chirring and chirruping around her, the echoing lament of a cuckoo, the peep-peep and rapid cascading notes of a wren defining its territory. An iridescent blue arrow darts through the air, just above her head, as a kingfisher navigates its way back to its mate.

Stepping dreamily through gossamer blades of grass, sparkling with diamond dew, she drifts through a bounteous fruiting orchard of quince, pomegranate, fig, and mulberry. Everywhere she looks, exotic and luscious fruit ripen on laden trees and bushes.

With a sharp snap, she plucks a pistachio nut from a nearby tree causing it to shake in irritation, and rustle its leaves threateningly. This sudden, unexpected noise startles a nearby white-bodied crane, which bustles away down to the stream in consternation. A louder rustling to her left makes her jump and, turning round, she sees a shaggy brown boar emerging unceremoniously from the undergrowth. Approaching Jae, it gives her trainers a desultory sniff before wandering benignly away, fully occupied with its own business.

Jae's heart overflows with happiness at being here, in the most glorious garden she's ever seen, so full of life, unspoilt and fertile.

Taking a deep breath of dampened air she decides to head away from the stream, dipping down to pass underneath a gnarled grape vine - bulging purple grapes dangling succulent and alluringly near her head. Then, to her complete surprise, she emerges into a clearing and finds herself standing in front of a magnificent wide stone circle, composed of large T-shaped pillars, standing about six metres high. Carved into each of the flat sides are three dimensional images of exotic animals, such as cranes, ducks and wild geese, as well larger beasts such as lions, boars, and crocodiles. The reliefs appear to be recently chiselled, exhibiting detailed depictions of animals that probably live in the near vicinity. *Lions and crocodiles?* Jae looks around in sudden anxiety, but sees nothing to alarm her. The trees and undergrowth remain peaceful, calm and still.

Wandering in awe slowly between the stone pillars, absorbing everything, she notices additional representations of gazelles, goats, foxes, snakes, scorpions, and many other small creatures. Although these elaborate reliefs undoubtedly portray the full bounty of local wildlife, that seems to be all. Jae can't spot any mysterious symbols, writing, or carvings of men or women. Due to their T-shape, she thinks the megaliths look like stylised trees, or maybe even human beings themselves. She wonders what their purpose could be, standing immobile and silent in such a perfect circular formation.

Inside the stone circle is a floor constructed of burnt lime and clay. Passing into the very middle, she sits carefully down to think and fully appreciate the setting. *Am I inside a building without a roof? On burial ground, or in a place of worship? Is this, perhaps, a mausoleum or temple..?* Lying down on her back and gazing up into the hazy blue sky, she watches the outlines of branches swaying lazily in the gentle breeze, their fruit dangling temptingly towards her. She thinks, *whatever it is, this is a sanctuary of profound beauty.*

Stretching out her limbs she sighs with pleasure and gratitude, a few fallen leaves and a granule or two of earth attaching themselves to her hair and clothes.

The smell of fresh soil and foliage, combined with her complete isolation in this verdant warm land, is rich and seductive. She idly strokes her fingers over the surface of the lime floor, scattered with detritus from nearby plants and vegetation. She feels drowsy, intangibly connected on a spiritual level to her surroundings, and perfectly relaxed.

Lazily turning her head to the left she gazes once more, with half-closed eyes, at the carvings on the insides of the pillars… and notices, this time, that they're not images at all, but some kind of writing. Sitting up in surprise, she brushes the leaves and earth from her jacket and gets to her feet, thinking she must be mistaken. However, on closer inspection, she sees there are indeed words, and what's more, they're written in a language she can understand without effort.

Wide-eyed and greatly intrigued, she reads aloud the sentence inscribed on the stone in front of her: 'Seek and ye shall find.'

It seems that this sanctuary is the guardian, perhaps source, perhaps ending, of her journey. Words from millennia ago from a teacher in a distant land passed down through the generations, and her grandmother's life and death - words powerful enough to change her life - are engraved here in stone at the heart of this extraordinary garden. And yet reading them now, unlike before, she no longer feels confused, provoked, or incited to urgent action. Instead, they comfort and reaffirm her in the present moment.

She nods with respect and walks over to the next

pillar in the circle, which also has writing carved on the inside surface. It simply asks: 'Who am I?'

She responds viscerally to this most ancient yet familiar question about the individual human mind. It is to here that 'seek and ye shall find' has ultimately guided her; a place awaiting anyone who recognises that the unexamined life is not worth living. Her journey has taught her that it is a deadly serious question which encompasses all others, a question which has led her from an ordinary life back to an ordinary life, through a profound shaking of the foundations of her identity.

With open and appreciative expectation, she walks over to the third pillar and reads aloud the four words inscribed in front of her: 'Not this, not that.'

Her guardian pillars are apparently forbidding any conceptual hiding place. The self is nothing, not this, not that - not thought, not no-thought. Awareness was always there, merely overcome by the din of the search party. It's a beautiful and utterly serious koan, a constant guide to the right use of mind; and a gift from a different teacher in another culture, but one with which Jae no longer needs to struggle. She now understands that there is no need to continue trying to bash her head against a brick wall, when neither wall, nor head, exists.

With another nod of respect, she approaches the fourth pillar, which asks her, 'By what authority?'

It is a seemingly straightforward question, but Jae at once recognises one of the essential tools which has brought her to this ecstatic space. Throughout her life, as most people do, she's been accumulating layers of assumptions and beliefs from one authority or another. This simple question is an unstoppable instrument of demolition, one which she will never again be without.

Still at ease amongst these astounding pillars engraved with language which, not long ago, would have completely baffled her, she approaches the fifth stone column. Carved in four descending lines, she reads the words: 'The first step is the last step. The seeker is the sought.'

Jae's favourite poem has long been Eliot's 'Four Quartets,' and haunting lines from the last stanza imprinted themselves on her mind years ago:

> We shall not cease from exploration
> And the end of all our exploring
> Will be to arrive where we started
> And know the place for the first time.
> ......
> A condition of complete simplicity
> (Costing not less than everything)

Not metaphor, not poetic excess, she has now established this to be simple truth. The fervour of intelligent curiosity struggling free of the morass of social conditioning, and nurtured by her grandmother, was the catalyst that initially launched her search. And after everything unnecessary was burned away, the flame of awareness remains. Pure and incorruptible. No goal or God has been discovered, the flame itself suffices: the seeker is the sought.

With the poem running through her mind like a litany, Jae turns to the next column, reciting five simple words, a gift from a more recent teacher in her own culture: 'Truth is a pathless land.'

The pillars are releasing her from a world of

riddles and questions into a world of directly shared understanding, and seem to have an organic relationship with her soul. Unlike remote commandments handed down from some kind of exalted external authority, these are analogous to ten stone mirrors to her mind.

Not long ago, the phrase, 'truth is a pathless land,' was completely unacceptable to Jae, searching as she was, flat-out for truth. Now it is part of her core being. No net can trap the flowing life of the universe, no belief can map its paths. The truth of the present moment is a corollary of awareness, and she must be, and is, fully satisfied with this.

Embracing and assimilating this articulation, she understands that many people have journeyed here before her, leaving their way-markers... fingers pointing to the moon.

With a deep sense of undirected gratitude she walks over to the seventh pillar and sees a sentence she knows from her musical background: 'The highest purpose is to have no purpose at all.'

This used to confuse and annoy Jae, but now all her metaphysical purposes have been stripped away, it just seems to be a statement of the essence of the garden. Acknowledging the pillar as a friend, she moves along to the next, which states: 'To live at all is miracle enough.'

She knows, and has always loved, this simple saying. It seems to carry its own charge of peace to a mind desperate for answers. Joy without motive, not purchased in the marketplace bartered and exchanged for some kind of need. If only this were widely and deeply comprehended in our culture, what a transformation might follow!

With a sigh she walks on, noticing she's almost come full circle back to the first pillar, and for the first time amidst this affirmative celebration - this feast for the return of a lost sheep - she begins to feel a tinge of apprehension. The air has become colder by a few degrees, and it seems to be getting darker. As she approaches pillar number nine in the fading light, she reads the inscribed words, 'To be is to be related.'

The apprehension was justified. Whilst she can now accept the validity of this challenge, which dismisses all the ways in which the self seeks identity on its own terms, it is no longer enough to acknowledge the stones gratefully from the security of this sanctuary. Just as a sub-atomic particle takes its nature from the sum of its interactions with other particles and fields, so Jae has parents, a daughter, and possibly a partner, who call her back into real time. Her insights can be tested and proved to be valuable only in a life open to the whole range of human emotion and suffering.

Her unease deepening, suddenly she feels nervous about reading the words on the final pillar. What could be more profound than everything she has experienced and already understood? Why should she fear anything now? Is there some unexplored obstacle that she still needs to vanquish, some remnant of blindness, some crafty technique of self-deception that she hasn't yet addressed? Could she so quickly have become attached again, this time to the bliss of the sanctuary..?

Mouth set firmly, she takes a few steps… and now the last pillar is directly in front of her. Taking a steadying breath she allows her eyes to rest upon the final expression, and fearfully reads, 'What's wrong mummy?'

Gasping in surprise and staggering backwards, she feels something implode deep within her body. She shouts loudly and passionately into the gloom, "nothing is wrong, darling, nothing is wrong, I promise…" Her voice echoes into the woody air but is immediately swallowed up, leaving her feeling impotent and alone. Feeling an overwhelming urge to return home without delay, to care for Chloe and to live fully in the real world, she cries out once more, urgently and passionately, "I'm coming..!" frantically scanning from left to right, trying to decide which way to run. But she can't make up her mind. *I need to get home right now,* she thinks desperately, *but which is the right way?*

Finally she decides to go east. But as she sets off, immediately encounters a strong wind that thrusts and pushes against her body, hampering her movements and preventing her from making much headway. Hunching forwards she attempts to run into the powerful air current… but it's difficult to make any significant advance, and soon she begins to doubt she's made the right choice.

Is the wind trying to tell me something? she wonders; however a small, stubborn voice in her mind urges her to stay strong and continue in her chosen direction. Somehow she knows she is on the right course for home. But the confusing thing is, the faster she attempts to run, the more slowly she seems to move through space, until it's almost as if she's just floundering on the spot. Nonetheless, she refuses to give up, and is relieved to see that she must have been making some kind of progress because the landscape around her has changed.

As the gale begins to subside from hurricane strength to a more manageable gusty wind, she examines her surroundings for any helpful or familiar landmarks. She can't see very far ahead in the twilight but the terrain is pretty barren and desolate, with just the occasional solitary tree sparing the view from being completely bleak. The wind gusts little clouds of dust into her face and she turns away, shielding her face with her arms, to find shelter under the nearest tree.

By now it's almost night again. A high half-moon produces enough radiance to allow her to navigate towards a massive, ancient bristlecone pine tree situated not far from where she's standing. Squat and truncated, yet at the same time extraordinarily majestic, these trees are said to be among the oldest living organisms in the world. Approaching reverentially, Jae recalls watching a recent television programme explaining that some bristlecone pines have lifespans of up to five thousand years, and potentially even longer. This one looks as if it could be a Bronze Age conifer itself, alive before the pyramids of ancient Egypt were built, and she admires it in spite of her predicament.

Although it affords her little respite from the wind, she feels safer standing next to the tree's thick, twisting trunk - a solid, immovable companion in this strange forsaken land - its heavy load of needles rustling unceasingly above her in the blustery wind. Staring out beyond the farthest branches Jae is surprised to discover a carved wooden fence crossing the landscape. Moving closer, she stares in surprise at the sight of angels, cherubim, and all kinds of strange mythical and spiritual creatures sculpted onto the panels. Following it visually from one end to the other, as far as her eye can see, she detects no gateways or gaps through the fence.

There appears to be no possibility to pass through, although she knows intuitively that she must continue beyond it in order to reach home.

As she stands wondering what to do, with the wind grabbing roughly at her hair and clothes, and eddies of dust swirling past her legs, she slowly starts to sense a presence, as if something not quite material has emerged menacingly out of the wind, to block or challenge her way forward.

Squinting into the gloom, she can vaguely distinguish a flickering glow to the left of the bristlecone, directly in front of the fence. Moving cautiously back round the tree, she becomes aware of an inwardly collapsing space forming in the air, a kind of compacted, nebulous whirlwind about twice her height, fizzing portentously. It is the colour of burnished bronze and emits little flashes of amber and gold as it swirls and convulses just a short distance in front of her. She can't so much see, as feel its presence, although as she peers anxiously through the wind and dust, she realises she can now detect the shape of a terrifying creature within the cyclone. It appears to have four massive faces, four powerful wings, the body of a gigantic bull, and the arms and hands of a male human. And she can unmistakably see that each face takes on a different form: that of a human, an ox, an eagle, and a lion.

An original cherub! A monstrous half-human, half animal guardian! Jae blanches, recoiling in dismay, with no idea how she might run away, hide, or vanquish it and get past. Glancing round in a panic all she can see is the bristlecone pine tree looming silent and serene in the darkness. How could the tree help? Perhaps she could climb up and launch herself over the fence above the cherub to the safety of the other side? But she immediately dismisses the idea as ludicrous. The cherub would swallow her as she sailed through the air, or she'd break her legs as she landed on the other side, or she might smash into the fence and fall helpless at its feet. She has to find another way.

Staring wildly at the tree she spots something she hadn't previously noticed: a slim, elongated object balanced on its lower branches which she must have previously assumed to be a bough. Moving closer she's surprised to see a long, heavy-looking implement - a metal pole or possibly a sword in a scabbard - with a kind of handle or hilt sticking out towards her. Reaching up on tiptoes she folds her right hand around the extended grip, realising incredulously that the object is indeed a sword, and carefully removes it from its sheath. As she does so it spontaneously ignites with bright orange flames licking out in all directions from the blade. Grasping it tightly with both hands, her heart pounding, Jae holds it out in front of her at head height, turns and advances determinedly towards the cherub.

Suddenly, a loud, clear voice issues from the shifting indeterminate mass guarding the fence (or is it watching over the tree? Jae thinks fleetingly), "I guard the way to the place you wish to go. If you are resolved and true you will pass." The cherub doesn't solidly remain in the world, but fades in and out of focus, as if composed only of shadows and dust.

"Yes! I will pass," Jae shouts back, confidence flooding her veins as the wind whips her hair away from her face in tangled strands. "Nothing can distract me! I'll take this sword and it will always be with me in everything I do and everything I say."

Spitting dust from her mouth and narrowing her eyes, she daringly draws closer to the cherub, the flaming sword outstretched in front of her. Although frightening to look at, Jae realises that it doesn't seem to threaten her with any immediate harm.

Once again it speaks, "taking this sword with you into the world means you will never entirely conform. You'll lose friends and may often feel isolated and lonely. You'll perpetually find yourself confronting difficult situations where you will be the only person with your point of view, yet you'll feel compelled to state it nonetheless. It will seem as if you're always going against the grain, making many people feel uncomfortable. Many times you'll be the only one propounding certain actions, the only one to dare to declare the truth when all others in the room would rather the falsification."

Jae answers in a high, determined voice, "I understand. But I won't change my mind. I'll take this sword and will wield it, no matter what it costs. I'll always bear it. From now on I am the sword!"

And with that she charges forward with a great challenging cry, slashing at the guardian with her fiery blade. But in that moment the swirling cyclone containing the monster instantly dissolves as if it were never there in the first place. Instead the sword crashes down onto a panel of the wooden fence intricately decorated with angles, splintering the designs and breaking the wood. Orange sparks from the sword fly out into the black night air as she raises it once more, bringing it violently down on the broken piece of fence. As the panel collapses to the ground she lunges through the gap, turning sharp left, and runs headlong into the darkness on the other side. She notices gratefully that as she runs, the sword begins to feel lighter and is easier to carry in just her right hand.

After running for a while without any signs of being chased, she slows to a light jog, and eventually a brisk walk. Panting and gazing firmly ahead, she begins to make out a dim light in the distance. Taking this as her guide she continues purposefully towards it, feeling hopeful and optimistic. Soon she recognises the familiar outline of the lamppost that stands at the edge of the garden. Turning left once more, she hurries along the side of the house, reaching the front door with sweat cooling on her brow.

Catching her breath, she lifts her right hand to examine the sword, which now feels so light as to be almost non-existent, but sees only her front door key clutched tightly in her fingers. Sliding it into the lock, she enters the house with a weary but untroubled sigh.

Inside, Jae places the key on the kitchen table, fetches a glass from the cupboard and fills it with water. Padding straight upstairs to Chloe's bedroom, she sets the glass on her bedside table and kneels on the floor, gently hugging the slumbering child. Inhaling her hot sleepy smell and enfolding her tenderly in her arms, she stays like this for a while, until at last Chloe stirs and pushes her softly away. Jae is filled with an immense feeling of love for her daughter, and gratitude that they are both alive and healthy. Every moment of existence is another moment in paradise.

Eventually, leaving the little girl to sleep in peace, she heads along the landing to her own bedroom. Before taking her clothes off and sinking into bed, she stares into the grey and white octagonal mirror hanging over the fireplace on the wall. It presents a crystal-clear reflection of her face: straggly, dark brown hair flowing down beyond her shoulders, brown eyes full of depth and understanding and an overriding expression of contentment.

I must rest now, she thinks, and lifting back the duvet sinks into bed falling almost immediately into a deep sleep.

CHAPTER TEN

In the World

Waking up the next morning and staring out of the bedroom window, Jae feels a surge of delight as she stares at the fully blossoming magnolia tree in the front garden. The striking goblet-shaped flowers seem themselves to radiate pastel pink sunlight; an enchanting vision of soft-hued creams and muted pinks. It's a glorious and exhilarating sight that will greet her every morning for the next two or three weeks. Jae thinks, *it's so exquisite it's like waking up in the very Garden of Eden.*

Turning away with a happy sigh, she collects her iPad from the bedside table and goes downstairs to make a cup of tea. Padding into the kitchen she's confronted by the unexpected sight of a large puddle of soapy water discharging from the bottom of the washing machine. Chucking her iPad on the kitchen table she rushes back upstairs to the airing cupboard to fetch some towels and soak up the mess. The washing machine seems to be stuck mid-cycle, door firmly locked, and for some unknown reason is leaking all over the kitchen floor. Kneeling on one of the few dry tiles in her pyjamas, she constructs a towel boom, slowly drawing it inwards to absorb the slick. Poking towels under the cupboard adjacent to the machine she soaks up the water hiding beneath, and to her amazement they come out not only wet, but black with dirt, grease, and dust.

"Ugh, disgusting!" she mumbles, executing an arabesque as she regains the only dry floor tile.

After she's cleaned up the water and squeezed the towels out into the bath upstairs, she tugs once more at the washing machine door, but it still doesn't budge. *We'll have to call someone,* she concludes knowing when to give up.

Boiling the kettle for tea and putting bread in the toaster, she begins a peaceful breakfast alone with her iPad. Checking her Facebook newsfeed she sees an addition to the comments on her previous status of 'hello world.' Justin has written 'hello Jae.' With a little rush of joy she understands he's reaching out to her, and is probably ready to talk. Perhaps later today? Or maybe tomorrow? *Whenever he's in the mood, I'll be here.*

Jae 'Likes' Justin's comment.

After finishing her breakfast she goes upstairs to Chloe's bedroom and gently hugs her daughter into consciousness. "Time to wake up now my darling. Leaving for school in forty-five minutes."

A little later, having written a note to her parents about the washing machine, she and Chloe walk briskly to school enveloped in bright yellow sunshine.

Strolling unhurriedly back home along the river, Jae reflects on how changed she feels. She fully recognises that after the death of Vivian she'd started to live almost entirely inside her questions, neither enjoying life nor properly interacting with other people. Justin must have found her distant, preoccupied, possibly even cold. But she's grateful that least she hadn't got to the stage of repressing her troubles and masking them off from her consciousness by drinking, taking drugs, or becoming obsessed with something. Nonetheless, she can admit that she had become inattentive, difficult to handle and removed from the present. She sees this now, in hindsight. Friends had occasionally asked her if anything was wrong, commenting that she seemed quieter than usual, but she'd brushed their concerns aside preferring to act as if everything was normal. At first they'd been forgiving in the knowledge that she'd just lost a close family member, but when her brooding, pensive mood continued long after it would reasonably have been expected to rally, they'd steadily started to withdraw, and eventually stopped contacting her altogether.

Through her journey – searching, thirsting, yearning; realising that the many questions were fundamentally only one question, wrestling and battling with the self, reaching a peak of presumed understanding, descending the peak to set aside the ego, and ultimately the guidance and comfort of the path itself, before finally realising that everything is already perfect... she meets the underlying question with the realisation that the seeker is the sought. The truly serious question, once attended to deeply, and stripped of all complexity and obfuscation, becomes its own answer. It's not a matter of being slightly tweaked or improved, sometimes able to see things from a different point of view; but rather it's a permanent severing of a blinding condition that, once removed, allows for a penetrating and previously unimaginable faculty of perception that can never be reversed. Jae knows she is a different person from the one she was before, but that this different person is, in fact, merely the rediscovery of the original person she was from the very beginning.

Standing still and gazing out over the fields resplendent in bright morning luminescence, she thinks, *there is nothing more to bother about.*

Jae arrives home to find her parents standing in the kitchen in their dressing gowns, discussing what to do about the broken washing machine. Her mother wants to buy a new one but her father thinks the current appliance should be kept and mended. Jae offers to phone a white goods repair company and describe the situation to ascertain whether it's worth fixing. Her parents gratefully accept.

"If it's any more than fifty pounds we may as well get a new one," shouts Jae's mother as she reaches for the phone.

"Nonsense!" exclaims her father, "that'll be the price purely for the initial call-out, not including parts and any labour beyond the first hour."

Jae ventures, "a decent new washing machine might cost two-hundred-and-fifty to three hundred quid, so maybe it's a question of deciding to pay between less than a hundred for a repair - which may not last that long - or about three hundred for a new one that'll probably last the rest of your lives."

"I plan to live a lot longer than fifteen more years thank you very much!" snaps her mother.

"Mum, I didn't mean that… machines these days can last a lot longer than…"

"Do you want **me** to make the call?" Jae is interrupted as her mother impatiently flaps a hand towards the receiver, "here, give me the phone."

"No, it's okay, I'm doing it right now," she answers, resigned.

After speaking with the repair company they establish that the call-out will cost forty-five pounds and any extra time, over and above the first hour, will be charged at thirty-five pounds per hour, although they suspect the leak is most likely to be solved within the hour. If any parts are needed they would have to pay for these too. Reluctantly agreeing that having the machine mended would probably be the more economical solution, in spite of the fact that it's already fifteen years old, her mother sweeps out of the room and moodily heads upstairs to get dressed.

Rolling his eyes to the ceiling Jae's dad grimaces as he re-boils the kettle.

There's no getting away from the hustle and bustle of real life, thinks Jae, giving her father a conspiratorial smile. *It's here every day, it goes on unstoppably. Problems arise and have to be dealt with.*

Going upstairs to her bedroom she roots around in the cupboard until she finds the pastoral painting she had taken down from the wall a few days earlier. She decides there's no point in keeping such a pleasant piece of art hidden away. She takes it back into the hall and re-hangs it where it was originally displayed. *I'm really rather fond of it now,* she thinks. Taking a little step back she admires it once more. Douke and the ox continue to tramp together through flowering pastures, unceasingly walking the path, on their way to nowhere.

Later that evening she drives to choir practice in the next town, borrowing her mother's car as usual. She greets friends as she arrives, and smiles at the conductor, before finding her usual seat next to Aadita, second row from the front in the soprano section.

"Oooh, you look happy," exclaims her friend, "what happened?!"

Jae sticks her tongue out. "Cheeky. Well actually I am feeling happy, despite the fact that Justin and I broke up."

"Really? No! You're perfect for each other. What did you do?"

"Nothing. Behave woman!" Jae gives her a mock smack on the arm. "Well ok, I... if you want to be serious about it, it's a bit complicated. As you probably noticed, I've been a bit preoccupied since I lost my grandmother a couple of months ago. It really affected me deeply..." Jae's tone becomes suddenly serious and Aadita gently squeezes her arm.

"I'm sorry."

"It's okay. I haven't told you this before, but... she left me a note along with the money."

"A note? What did it say?"

Jae glances around the hall noticing that most people have now arrived, although the conductor is still occupied talking to the repetiteur. When he's ready to begin he'll just suddenly raise his hands and won't wait for everyone to then put on their glasses, turn off their mobiles, get their music out and turn to the right page. Jae doesn't want to be caught on the hop, so she rummages around in her bag for the score and opens it on her lap as she continues to speak to Aadita. "Well it was a bit strange, and it made me go into a sort of weird questioning state, not depression exactly, but restless and distracted. I kept thinking about the note all the time. I couldn't get it out of my mind…"

"Yes, but what did it say?!" repeats Aadita in an urgent undertone, dying to know.

Jae replies, staring straight into Aadita's eyes. "Seek and ye shall find."

"Seek and he shall find…? That's strange. Find what?"

"No, not 'he', '**ye**,'" corrects Jae, "seek and ye shall find. It's a quote from the Bible."

Just then the conductor claps his hands loudly for silence in the room.

"But you're not religious!" hisses Aadita holding her score up to her mouth to disguise her lips moving. "And neither was she if I remember correctly? Very mysterious. What does it mean..?"

"Tell you later," Jae whispers back, turning to give the conductor her full attention. It's a disadvantage if you miss the announcement of which page to start from. It means you spend the first few minutes tapping the people in front of you on the shoulder and mouthing, "which page?" with a desperate expression on your face.

After the warm-up, the conductor unexpectedly tells the choir to mix themselves up and sing from somewhere they've never stood before next to someone they've never spoken to. Jae secretly likes this technique because she's usually put enough time into studying the piece at home and can roughly sing her own part without prompts from those around her. Aside from this, when standing next to a different voice part, assuming they sing correctly, it can assist tuning and create a better overall blended sound. For people wedded to the comforting and familiar routine of standing in the same place beside the same people at every rehearsal, suddenly being asked to sing from a different location creates a palpable aura of dismay. Groans, complaints, and mock horrified laughter can be heard going round the room like a Mexican wave, as people resentfully push back their chairs and shuffle sideways along their rows to foreign ground. Jae quickly makes her way to the opposite side of the room and stands in the back row, a bass on her right and an alto on her left.

Jae smiles at both, and the grey-haired bass extends his hand with a smile, "Hi, I'm John."

"Jae. I hope I don't put you off!"

"Highly unlikely," replies John with a grin, "I don't know it very well so I'll be singing **really** quietly."

The conductor claps his hands once more for silence, interrupting the choir as they chatter excitedly to their new neighbours, prompting them to settle down and prepare to sing.

During the break, as Jae heads off to the loo, John catches up with her just before she leaves the main hall.

"How could you think I would put you off?!" he says admiringly, "you sing very confidently, and, I might add, mostly the right notes."

"Mostly?" Jae raises an eyebrow sardonically, "I was note perfect – although perhaps not for this piece."

"Funny," John replies with a chuckle. "You remind me of my daughter; although I think she's much younger."

"Thank you. I think," Jae replies. "I suppose she is similarly talented and good looking..?"

"Of course. Although, between you and me, she's a bit more wilful and headstrong than I'd like."

"Isn't that standard for daughters these days?"

"I don't know. Perhaps. It's just that we're having a particularly turbulent time with her at the moment." John immediately looks sheepish, glancing around the room as if he's accidentally revealed something secret and of great importance.

Jae's tone changes to one more serious. "A struggle?"

"Well... it's nothing really. I don't know why I'm telling you all this. I'm sure you don't want to listen to my trifling problems..."

"No, go on. I'm interested. What do you mean 'a turbulent time'?"

"Well... more like a battle of wills. She's very opinionated, headstrong; she just won't see life from my point of view."

"What do you mean?"

"Well, without wanting to get into too much detail, I'm a Roman Catholic, as is my wife, and we're trying to educate the children in line with our faith, but no matter what we do she's simply not interested. I keep suggesting she come along to church with us, but she always makes excuses. It's such a shame."

Jae appraises the older man. He must be in his sixties; he's tall, slim and well-dressed. She asks, gently, "why do you want her to have your views especially? Can she not have her own? Would you not consider letting her find her own ideology?"

"But it's the way I was brought up! I want my children to have the same comfort from Catholicism as I did, and still do. Catholicism, for me, is the guardian of the truth, the only proper way in which to live life, a pathway to the highest mind of man guided by God... I'm sorry, I don't know why I'm suddenly saying all this to you." He stops, perplexed, hearing himself overstepping the boundary of casual conversation and straying into the realms of moralistic preaching.

Jae smiles reassuringly, "it's fine, don't worry. You're only responding in such detail because I'm interested, I'm encouraging you. I'm at least fifty percent to blame! But, going back to the issue of belief, instead of trying to coerce or force your daughter into going to church, how about just going about your business, enjoying your life, gaining comfort from your faith and all that it gives you... and allowing your daughter to make up her own mind based on what she observes of your behaviour?"

"Well..."

"Don't you think it would be better if she came to Catholicism of her own free will without having to be persuaded? If you role model the behaviour you want to see in her, perhaps she would be much more open to experiment? If she can see how much you gain from being involved in Catholicism she may also want to try it. Then she'll be coming with you of her own accord, enquiringly, hopefully maybe; rather than resentfully and by persuasion. A curious, open mind is a much better way to approach religion than a closed, resentful mind, don't you think?

"Well yes, that's a very good point," John admits. "I could… I might try your 'softly, softly' method. For some reason I hadn't considered that before. We've been very concerned to get Rosie to church as soon as we could." He smiles nervously across the room at a friend who's staring at him quizzically.

Jae smiles directly at him, pleased to have been of use, uncaring about what on-lookers might be thinking. "Myself, I feel that religion hinders a person from seeing the truth, rather the opposite of what you've just said. But there may be a way of living a religious life in a non-religious way…"

"Well, thank you Jae. I'll consider that!" he laughs kindly. And as an afterthought he suddenly says, "you seem very self-contained."

"I'm happy," she answers simply, turning on her heel and walking back to her place. The break is over, and most people are already sitting back in their seats ready for the second half.

"Where've you been?" squeaks Aadita impatiently, "I've been waiting here all this time. You took ages in the loo. Do you think you might need to eat more vegetables?"

"I didn't get there!" Jae laughs, "I was waylaid. Got talking to the bass I stood next to earlier."

"Ooh, is he good looking?"

"Tsk! He's about as old as my dad. We were just talking. He's worried about his daughter not believing in God…"

"Oh boy!" Aadita rolls her eyes, "and talking of God, what about that note your granny left you. I still want to know! What does it mean?"

"Okay, if you insist. I think she was hinting for me to find meaning in my life, to answer some important questions she knew were bothering me."

Seeing a puzzled expression come over her friend's face, Jae continues, "you know how in ancient times people used to undertake long journeys, spiritual pilgrimages, to a special church or famous location where there was a holy relic? Well, I sort of did that myself, but in a way that didn't involve organised religion or belief. It was an inner journey, a personal revelation. And at the end of my journey I found… I found…" Jae sighs searching for a way to put into words that she had found nothing, no answers at all, just a vanishing of self - a complete release of attachment and a new aware observation in the moment. "I found…"

"Yes? You found what? A crown of thorns? A massive bar of chocolate? The solution to world peace?

Jae laughs. "Yes all of that. But mainly I found inner peace."

"Hmmm," Aadita appraises her friend thoughtfully. "You're just getting old."

"Absolutely," Jae grins, as the conductor raises his voice over the din to welcome the choir back from their break.

After choir is over Aadita and Jae help carry and stack chairs in the hall, before saying their goodbyes until next week. Walking out into the car park Jae switches her phone back on and a new text message announces itself. Justin would like to meet up with her tomorrow for a quiet walk and to talk things through. She replies at once, suggesting they meet at the kissing gate in a particular field near the river – a place they've often been to together in the past.

The next day Jae is at the gate first. It's mid-morning and bright and sunny. She's wearing denim shorts and a pale blue short-sleeved top with her usual beige trainers. Her shining brown hair is gathered up into a long pony tail which swings over her back. A gorgeous spring day is materialising. As she stands casually leaning on the gate appreciating the view, a dazzling yellow male brimstone butterfly lands on the post and basks in the sunshine. "You and me both," says Jae companionably, "this is your ascendancy, your zenith. You have fully flowered…"

"Talking to nobody again?" Justin laughs as he approaches, seeing her standing alone muttering. "You always were a bit strange."

"Well, I've changed completely," she answers affectionately, "now I'm **very** peculiar."

"Well, I love you the way you are."

"Really?" She looks at him steadily. His blond hair is styled back from his face, the same as it always was, but he's let stubble grow on his chin and he looks older. He is wearing slightly grubby jeans and a close-fitting brown t-shirt that flatters his slender frame.

He appraises her sincerely, hazel eyes glittering. "Yes, really."

At this, Jae moves towards him and they embrace passionately. Birds call excitedly from the nearby hedgerows startled by their sudden movement.

Hugging him tightly she closes her eyes, her mind empty, stroking his back with her hands.

"I've missed you," he murmurs into her ear; and then after a pause, "where have you been?"

Gently they release each other and turn to walk hand-in-hand along the track that leads to the river. Eventually it will join up with the same path that Jae followed on the day she resolved to end her questioning beyond doubt.

Taking a deep breath, she begins. "First I have to explain something important to you, and then I hope you will understand a bit better."

"Okay," Justin agrees, "I'm listening. I want to understand."

"What you don't know is that when granny died, as well as the money, she left me a note. It said, 'seek and ye shall find."

"Seek and ye shall find? Isn't that from the Bible?"

"Yes. I've since looked it up. It's from Matthew. The whole quote goes something like, 'Ask, and it shall be given to you; Seek, and ye shall find; Knock, and it shall be opened unto you.' It's really incredibly beautiful."

"But you're an atheist, aren't you? And so was Vivian…"

"No, I'm not an atheist, I'm agnostic if you must have a label," she smiles.

"Oh, all right."

"Good." She gently rests her head briefly on his shoulder, "because there's a huge difference between the two. Anyway, before she died, Vivian and I had been exploring issues of meaning and spirituality in life generally. As you know, we used to sit drinking tea in the conservatory together, talking for hours. My central problem was that I felt I lacked meaning and spirituality in my life, and I'd started to wonder whether religion would provide me with the answer, like mum and dad have Christianity. Vivian argued against this, speaking more abstractly about things like 'emptiness' and 'self-vanishing' which I couldn't understand, but I was very intrigued by. I think she had some kind of exceptional wisdom, and I don't just mean the banana cake recipe."

Justin concedes, "it was delicious."

"But seriously, I believe she knew something terribly important that couldn't be expressed in words, and was trying to hint at it in her note. Before that, we were merely going round and round, weaving webs with words, not getting very far. I was constantly questioning her, and I think that was a cause of frustration because I kept putting her in the position of having to provide answers – which she usually avoided doing, but which in turn only further stoked the vigour of my enquiries!"

The sudden call of a skylark stops them in their tracks, and they squint upwards to watch its vertical display flight and listen to its long, liquid warbling. Presently they continue along the path, and Jae resumes her explanation.

"Vivian hinted that if you really want it, there is a way to live a deeply spiritual life, a religious life, without the man-made organised religion we immediately associate it with; in fact, a life without beliefs of any kind at all. I'm not saying I understood all this at first, but I was deeply curious. The possibility excited me, and I started asking myself all sorts of serious and onerous questions. My plan was to come back to her the next time we met with a whole list of further proposals and thoughts... but she died before we could arrange anything. It hit me so hard for many reasons, but a large part of it was because we'd just started talking about a topic that was especially fascinating to me. I felt she knew something pivotal, something of great consequence, and I desperately wanted to explore what it was she had discovered. When she died I thought the discussion was lost to me forever. Until I received the note."

Jae becomes pensive, her heart filling with the pain of her recent loss and sadness at the memory of her disappointment. However she doesn't dwell on it for long and the mood soon passes. "But... it was never meant to be. And then... yes, the mysterious note! Vivian was thinking about me. I knew she wanted to encourage me. It was her way of throwing open the doors in my mind; of kick-starting me on the path to discovery."

The little track they're following ushers them round a bend and finally, they hear and see the river sparkling in the sunlight a few metres ahead. Merging with the main embankment path, they now follow in Jae's footsteps of several days ago, walking single file, the tall hedge to their left.

Suddenly Jae stops. "I think I'm not going to walk any further if that's okay? I might go back."

Justin nods and takes her hand in his, "no problem."

"Do you ever have questions, Justin? Like the ones I was wrestling with? Have you ever asked yourself whether life has a deeper meaning?"

To her surprise he answers in the affirmative, "yes I do, Jae. Quite often. But it doesn't consume me. It's not something urgent - a dire pressing need like it was for you. You know, I think most people probably do think about such things, consciously or unconsciously, at various times throughout their lives."

"Yes, I agree," Jae replies mildly. "I don't by any means think I'm unique."

She takes up his other hand, and looking intently into his eyes, makes a suggestion. "Why don't you continue along the path for a bit? It's such a beautiful day. I'll walk back and we can meet later at mine for coffee. Perhaps this afternoon we can both go and pick up Chloe together?"

He searches her eyes and finds nothing but sincerity and affection. "Okay. You know I love you, Jae, and want to be with you. Perhaps we can hatch a plan to live together again, just me, you, and Chloe."

Jae squeezes his hands tightly. "Yes I would really like that. In fact, I've already got an idea for a business I want to start. If I can make it work, maybe we'll have enough money, with your salary and my inheritance, to get our own two-bedroom flat and not have to panic about how to pay for it."

He takes her into his arms and they hug for a long time in silence, enjoying the closeness and comfort of each other's bodies, listening to the eternal noises of the countryside. Echoing cries of birds skim across the sky, the faint rumble of a bus reaches them from a distant road, and a fragrant breeze swishes through new leaves in the springtime hedgerow. Jae hopes that maybe, finally, they'll be able to commence a mature relationship; one without images, duplicity, or power games, with each seeing the other exactly the way they are in the present moment, hearing exactly what they are saying now, without the confusing interference of the twin autocrats of thought and ego. If they could accomplish this it would be a rare and wonderful achievement. Difficult, but not altogether impossible.

Eventually, stepping away with a little nod and a smile, Justin turns aside and continues alone along the footpath, towards the tall grasses at the water's edge and the open fields across the river.

"Later dude," Jae calls out to him softly, watching him disappear round the corner, "look out for the bridge…"

With a surge of contentment she turns back and heads for home.

Joining her parents for a light lunch of homemade watercress soup and bread, she explains her idea.

"I know what I want to do with granny's money…"

"Oh good," replies her father enthusiastically, "I'm so glad you've come to a decision."

"I'm going to start a business. I'm going to become a masseuse!"

"Massage?" exclaims her mother taken aback, "are you sure? But you don't know anything about it! Weren't you going to go into psychotherapy or counselling? Isn't that why you did your degree?"

Jae nods slowly. "I was, but after I've changed my mind. On reflection, I no longer believe it to be suitable. I'm going to enrol on a course - use some of the money to pay for that - and the rest to start the business."

She laughs with pleasure at their surprised faces. "I love it! I massage Justin all the time and he's often

213

said I have a natural aptitude."

But her mother interrupts, a concerned expression on her face, "but what about all the dodgy businessmen asking for extras?"

"Mum!" Jae exclaims, half amused. "Of course there may be some difficult customers, as I'm sure is the case in most professions, but it depends on where and how you advertise, and what kind of clinic you operate. There are ways and means to make it perfectly clear."

"Hmm."

"The benefits of massage are huge. There are studies to suggest massage may be helpful in treating insomnia, fibromyalgia, anxiety and stress, and of course all kinds of sports and accidental injuries. I think it'll be really fulfilling to be able to help people in this way."

"It's just a bit of a surprise, dear. It wasn't what we were expecting."

"I can't wait to start. Eventually I plan to have my own business. I've already found a course in town that I could apply for this summer."

After a short silence she asks, "what do you think?"

"Well I…" begins her father.

"If it's what you really want to do…" says her mother.

"It is," Jae replies firmly, "and I have a master plan. Justin and I will search for a two-bed flat together soon; not far away – we still need to get Chloe to school and back – but if I can use the money to help me live while I train to become a masseuse, I think together we can do it. You'd get your house back to yourselves, and we three would be living together as a family, but this time with enough space so we're not on top of each other… and I'll be starting my business."

After a pause her father reaches out and squeezes her shoulder. "I think that's a very good plan," he says affectionately. "We'll support you where we can, with childcare and babysitting, and so on."

"Thanks, dad. That's great. And very much appreciated." Jae beams at her parents, who she knows will need some time to get used the idea.

"Do you mind if I cut myself another slice of bread?"

"But of course not, you silly girl," her father replies incredulously, "no-one else has been doing that for you for at least two decades!"

Jae and her mother stare at him, dumbfounded.

"What on earth do you mean, dad?"

"Well obviously… hang on… didn't you just say, "do you mind if I tuck myself up in bed?""

Jae and her mother roar with laughter. "You madman!" It's definitely time to get a hearing aid!"

Her father joins in the general hilarity, apologising for his mistake and reluctantly admitting his hearing does seem to be getting worse. "Don't mock me, ladies, I can't help it. I live in a world where anyone can say anything, and sometimes I get caught out and forget to doubt."

"We forgive you, elderly pater," says Jae, gently patting his arm.

As they gradually calm down and resume eating, Jae watches her two parents as they sit at the kitchen table smiling and quietly eating their soup. They chew on slices of buttered bread, and every so often blot their mouths with a napkin. Simply looking at them makes her feel completely happy. Glancing out of the side window she sees a shaft of sunlight lingering on a peripheral twig of the magnolia tree, glorifying it in shimmering brilliance.

There is no difference between that twig and me, she thinks. *We are one and the same. And I and the sunlight are one...* Pushing back her chair and going over to the window for a closer look, she spots a beetle scuttling idly on a leathery petal. *The beetle and I are one.*

Finding immense value in her ordinariness, she is utterly grateful to be alive and partaking in the adventure of living as a normal human being, with all its attendant ups and downs, struggles and shocks, joys, ill-health, loves and boredom. Beyond sensation and need, unimpeded by illusion and deceit, clear thinking and incorruptible observation have transformed the potential drudgery of everyday living into something unique and sacred.

I am right back where I started, only now I have no questions at all. I do what I need to do, and say what I need to say... and the frogs continue to croak outside in the evening. How much effort was needed for this! From the very beginning, at the most basic level, I was complete and perfect, lacking nothing. This is the indisputable truth, hiding in plain view, obscured by its utter simplicity. And the secret beauty is that this perfection can only be revealed through personal verification, during the self-driven undertaking of secular pilgrimage.

She hears birds chirruping outside, hurrying about their business, attracting mates and building nests in readiness for the annual arrival of offspring. The birds are responsible only to themselves, getting on with life, doing what they need to do. Jae's responsibility to the world is borne out merely by being herself, like the birds - building a nest and going about her business; her sword tightly clasped in her hand.

Decoding

Chapter Two

The sculptor is based on Constantin Brâncuşi, a Romanian sculptor born in 1876 who made his career in France, and is considered a pioneer of modern sculpture.

The Humanists (Vice Presidents, and President, of the British Humanist Society in 2013:

Polly (Vice President Polly Toynbee)
Simon (Vice President Professor Simon Blackburn)
Mary (Vice President Mary Honeyball MEP)
Evan (Vice President Dr. Evan Harris)
Jim (President Professor Jim Al-Khalili)

The Existentialists:

Fred = Friedrich Nietzsche
John = Jean-Paul Sartre
Martin = Martin Heidegger

"the ladder on square number 80" refers to the original Spears' board game of snakes and ladders. Landing on number 80 is incredibly lucky – the player ascends straight to the winning square.

Douke - Kanji Symbols (Chinese characters used in Japanese writing): 'Dou' of the first character means 'a way', 'a load' or 'a street', and 'Ke' of the second character means 'disguise'. Douke can therefore mean 'a disguised way.' Alternative meanings for 'dou' and 'ke' are 'child' and 'play' together forming the phrase 'child's play.' It can also be translated into English as one word (rather than two separate ones) and means 'clown' ('pierrot' in Japanese). Douke is therefore the hidden way, the fool that speaks truth to power.

Chapter Three

The conductor is based on the 'Mad' Hatter from 'Alice's Adventures in Wonderland.'

'Sapere Aude' is Latin for 'dare to know.'

Florence Foster Jenkins was an amateur operatic soprano born in the mid-19th century who became convinced that she was a talented singer. In fact, she was known as one of the worst singers of all time and widely derided for her poor performances and lack of musical ability. There are a few recordings on YouTube.

The flowers in the vase on dressing room table are oxeye daisies.

The bottle of wine is Dancing Bull (Californian Zinfandel).

Chapter Five

Bliss Point – in processed food design, the 'bliss point' is the addition of the maximum amount of salt, sugar, and/or fat added to food before it becomes too sickly to eat.

Vesta – Ancient Roman goddess of hearth, home and family.

Freya – Norse goddess of love, beauty and fertility.

Demeter – ancient Greek goddess of the harvest, marriage, and the cycle of life and death. Virgin daughter Persephone was abducted to the underworld by Hades.

Tobiah – son of Tobit from 'The Book of Tobit.'

Ganapati – the Indian elephant-headed God, Ganesh.

Chapter Eight

This is the point at which identity disappears; a silent sacred space where heaven and earth and all in it and outside it are one. This experience can't be fully described in words, and is represented by a series of blank pages (apart from one line challenging the authority of the author).

Chapter Nine

"but *there* I have been" is a reference to a line from a T.S Eliot poem 'Burnt Norton.'

The words of the song in the garden are a translation of a version of a poem written by Ludwig Rellstab, set to the music of Schubert's famous 'Serenade.'

The stone circle in the Garden of Eden is based on Göbekli Tepe, a series of ancient limestone megaliths discovered in 1996, built approximately 11,600 years ago.

The Bristlecone pine represents the Biblical Tree of Life.

ABOUT THE AUTHOR

Jackie Griffiths has an MA in Psychoanalytic Studies and has been writing fiction and non-fiction material for twenty years. She founded an online copywriting business providing content for websites, print and digital media, before selling up to concentrate on her novels and short stories. She lives in the UK with her two children, and is currently working on her third novel.

30827442R00131

Made in the USA
Charleston, SC
27 June 2014